THE MIRACLE HOUR:

Predictable Sales in an Hour a Day

BY

KELLY ROACH

The Miracle Hour:
Predictable Sales in an Hour a Day

Published by: Motivation & Success Publishing (Motivation & Success, LLC).

Printed in the United States of America.

Cover design by Sean Foran.

ISBN:

979-8-234-00664-6 (ebook)
979-8-234-00900-5 (paperback)
979-8-234-00901-2 (audiobook)
979-8-234-01878-6 (hardback)

DISCLAIMER AND LEGAL NOTICES

The publisher and author have used their best efforts in preparing this book. However, they make no representations or warranties with respect to the accuracy, completeness, or suitability of the contents and specifically disclaim any implied warranties of merchantability or fitness for a particular purpose.

The advice, strategies, and information contained herein are provided for educational and informational purposes only. They are not intended as legal, financial, accounting, tax, or other professional advice. You should consult with a qualified professional before implementing any strategy discussed in this book.

Earnings & Results Disclaimer

Any income statements, revenue examples, testimonials, case studies, or financial representations referenced in this publication are provided for illustrative purposes only. They are not guarantees of income or performance. There is no assurance that you will achieve results comparable to those discussed in this book.

Business success depends on numerous factors including, but not limited to individual effort, experience, skill level, market conditions, timing, and the application of strategies. Because these factors vary widely among individuals and businesses, the publisher and author make no guarantee, representation, or warranty that you will achieve any particular result or earnings level.

Testimonials and case studies reflect the real-life experiences of individuals and businesses. In certain instances, names, identifying details, and specific business information have been changed to protect privacy and confidentiality. Individual results will vary.

"*The Miracle Hour* has helped us generate over seven figures in sales, not because of tricks or funnels but because it's human first. When you focus on real relationships, real conversations and real service, business growth becomes inevitable. It's simple and it works!"

— Maria Fontana, Founder at Maria Fontana Consulting

"*The Miracle Hour* gave me something I didn't even realize I was missing: direction. One focused hour of income-producing work each day has kept my business steady and growing, without the overwhelm. I used to feel scattered and pulled in a hundred directions. Now I know exactly what to start with, and that one hour leads my entire day. On the rare days I don't do it, I feel lost. That's how powerful this practice has been for me."

— Vennessa McConkey, Strategic Positioning Advisor

"*Miracle Hour* took the planning and mystery out of how to keep connected with clients and future clients — build consistency and predictability — thank you!"

— Lauren Chiren, CEO at Women of a Certain Stage

"Give your first hour to growth, and watch your whole life grow. This is what *Miracle Hour* did for me!"

— Carrie Richardson, Create Your Best Life Coaching

"*The Miracle Hour* helped me stop doing everything and start doing the right things. By focusing only on the true needle-moving activities, I began enrolling clients consistently and when I taught it to my team, I was able to duplicate my results through them. It didn't just improve my time management — it multiplied my impact."

— Charyse Williams, RN, Founder & Business Strategist for Functional Medicine Practitioners

To my husband, Billy, and my daughter, Madison:
You are the magic and miracles in my life.
We are rich because we have each other.

Contents

Chapter 1: The Miracle Hour Origin Story.. 11

Chapter 2: Reclaiming Control, One Hour at a Time 33

Chapter 3: The Millionaire Mindset: Beliefs That Generate Millions.... 61

Chapter 4: Take Back Your Most Important Asset: Your Time............. 77

Chapter 5: The Five Types of Sales Every Healthy Business Should Strive For 91

Chapter 6: The Seven Core Miracle Hour Activities That Make Daily Sales Possible.. 103

Chapter 7: Aligning Miracle Hour Activities With Your Growth Objectives 129

Chapter 8: Organize to Win 139

Chapter 9: Marketing is Not Sales 159

Chapter 10: The Five Phases of the Miracle Hour........................... 167

Chapter 11: Committing to Win: Mastering Daily Habits That Drive Predictable Growth 179

Chapter 12: Multiply and Scale 191

Chapter 1: The Miracle Hour Origin Story

Every miracle has an origin, and I hope and pray this book will be one for you. In my heart of hearts, after many years of teaching, coaching and training entrepreneurs of all walks of life, it has become crystal clear: You can transform any area of business or life in one, focused hour a day.

If something matters enough to you, there is always a way. Most entrepreneurs are overworked and underpaid. They sacrifice way too much and get too little. That stops here and now. This book is your line in the sand, it's your "no more" moment when you reclaim your power, take back your time and stop settling for anything less than what you deserve and desire in business and life.

After spending nearly a decade climbing the corporate ladder, being promoted seven times in eight years and building a team of 100 in 17 locations, I had mastered success but failed at fulfillment. I achieved my financial and career goals, but my heart and soul were suffering. I knew I was made for more. My time in the Fortune 500 world was challenging and sometimes frustrating but utterly life-changing. I received true mentorship and learned how billion-dollar companies run, operate and grow. It gave me the foundation to run my own companies and help others do the same. No regrets, no complaints. But there is a season and a reason for everything, and at a certain point, the impact of my work became far more important than the aesthetic of my career on paper. So it was time to begin again on my own terms, helping business owners like you stand on my shoulders. I decided I wanted to take what I had learned throughout my time in corporate and help everyday entrepreneurs grow and scale their own businesses, so that they could achieve financial freedom and fulfillment. This is where my journey as a business growth strategist and mentor began. There was just one problem.

While I would love to share a dramatic "I quit" moment and story of incredible overnight success after striking out on my own, it was nothing like that. You see, Billy (my husband and the love of my life) and I were in the process of architecting our dream life. We already knew that when we had a family someday, our child (or children) would be home with us, never in day care. We envisioned a freedom-based life where neither one of us had a job tying us down. We wanted to be truly *free*. This meant that while starting my "dream business" I would continue working my "day job."

My go-to in life has always been hard work. I was the first one in and the last one out every day, and I was rewarded for this. I never took a lunch break, often went into the office on the weekends and even sacrificed my social life, health and fitness goals, and beyond in order to go further, faster in my career.

This was not going to fly in this new paradigm of starting my own business while working full time. I was going to have no choice but to develop a completely new operating system. A system that did not rely on a number of hours to equate to results but instead on intent and impact. I share this with you as a potential inflection point in your own journey. If you feel as though you are sometimes overworked and underpaid, or working far more hours than what is truly reasonable long term, this is your invitation to a new way of thinking and being.

The truth is, usually the harder path is the right one in life, and I know this was the case for me. Most business owners jump to full-time entrepreneurship too soon and the business breaks. The average business takes over two years to produce enough revenue to actually support the business owner, and you must be able to reinvest to be successful. So even though the standard advice is to go all in, I don't believe that's the best strategy. Usually, I recommend keeping your day job until you can replace your full-time income with the business revenue and still have money to reinvest in growth.

As I was beginning to build my business, I started doing something I had never done before: Take a lunch break. Crazy, right?

I would go out to my little Jeep Liberty (a car I never loved but was a practical buy) on my lunch break for one hour a day. And in that hour each day, I built my bridge to freedom. Whether it was making calls to potential clients or following up with texts and emails, those seemingly small activities grew my tiny business into a seven-figure business. Within 18 months of becoming a full-time entrepreneur, I turned that into an eight-figure business. Fast forward to today: I now run a portfolio of companies. I broke my own "work harder, longer" paradigm and replaced it with a new one: You can change your life if you stay disciplined enough to commit one focused, intentional hour each day to making your dreams come true.

What can I do, where I am, with what I have? This is a huge life lesson and such an important mindset for entrepreneurs.

As an entrepreneur, it's tempting to compare yourself to others who have been in business longer — people with a bigger network, people who seem like they have more money or more access. In reality, every success that we have in life comes from taking the gifts that we've been given and putting them to work. From doing our best with integrity.

The Miracle Hour is about helping entrepreneurs around the world see that they can build their dream business. They can put their faith and family first. They can be successful as an entrepreneur. It's not about the number of hours you work. It's about the energy, intention, focus and discipline to do the right things at the right time in the right order to reach your goals. The results will astound you when you truly understand how to apply your very own Miracle Hour — whether it be for your business or life.

The Entrepreneurial Costs: Time and Money
Slack, a Salesforce company, conducted a study in 2024 showing that small businesses owners lose an average of 96 minutes of productivity each day, equating to about three weeks of lost time each year. 17% of those surveyed reported context switching as a top productivity killers (the average small business owner uses four different tools daily). I've spent over a decade helping people build seven- and eight-figure businesses online, and entrepreneurs always wonder why such a small percentage of small businesses make it to seven figures, let alone eight. I have done this for myself, and have helped others do the same, and here's what I've noticed: The average entrepreneur spends less than one hour a day performing profit-producing activities. Where are they wasting their time? On everything but the things that will get them to their goal.

Revenue Breakdown of U.S. Small Businesses

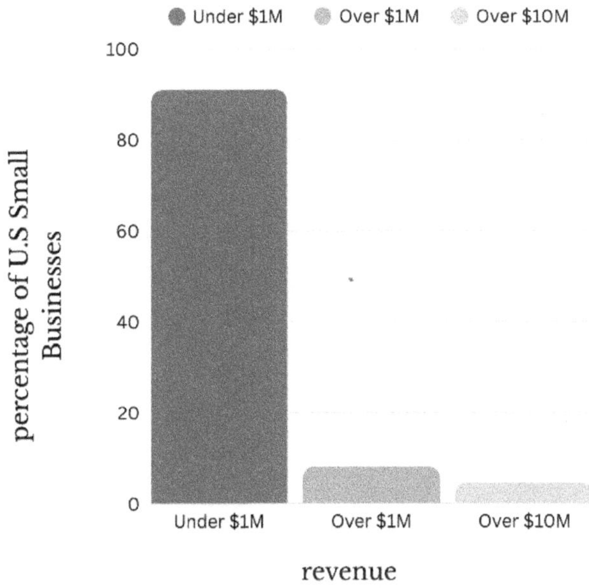

(source: unanswered (2026), circle of intrapreneurs (2025)

Figure 1.1

That's why I'm so passionate about helping businesses and teams leverage the Miracle Hour. If I could get millions of entrepreneurs to start focusing just *one hour a day* on profit-producing activities for their businesses, entrepreneurs around the globe would realize that they can stop compromising their fitness, health, passions, time with family and time for faith. Entrepreneurs think they must sacrifice every other part of their life to have a successful business. That's not true. But if you don't prioritize the *right* things, it will be true. Too often, entrepreneurs spend their time on things like productivity and tech tools that will supposedly save them time, consuming content from too many conflicting sources, constantly updating their websites and landing pages and on low-margin tasks that an administrative assistant should be doing for them — whether it's scheduling, rescheduling or putting out fires in the business because they don't have proper systems.

> *"The miracle hour worked miracles for me! It got me motivated and organized like no other "system" could. It's the structure I needed to be consistent and get results!"*
>
> *-Melissa Almon*
> *Strategy Advisor & Creative Director,*
> *Cowgirl Copy Studio*

There are two core things that make a business run well: getting clients and serving and retaining existing ones.

That's it.

Let's do a quick exercise together. Fill in the following chart to get organized. On the left side, list all the activities in your business that directly contribute to generating new clients or serving and retaining existing ones. On the right side, list *everything else* that you do day to day that takes up time in your business.

<table>
<tr><th colspan="2">Time Audit: Where Is Your Time Going?</th></tr>
<tr><td>ACTIVITIES DIRECTLY RELATED TO NEW CUSTOMER ACQUISITION, CUSTOMER SERVICE OR RETENTION:</td><td>ADDITIONAL TASKS:</td></tr>
</table>

Entrepreneurs constantly complain about how busy they are and how hard they are working. I get it. But the reality is that you have to make the *main thing* the main thing. Most people spend more time stressing about what they *want* to change than they do taking action to actually do something about it.

I'd venture to guess that most, if not all, of the things you wrote on the right side of the chart are important and meaningful in some way. That is not the point. The point is that you as the CEO (which should be spelled S-A-L-E-S, by the way) need to *lead*. That means being visible and focused on the things that makes it easier for your team to sell, market and serve for you.

It's time to start prioritizing the center of the flywheel: *acquiring customers* and *serving your existing ones*. It is human nature to do what we're comfortable with, what feels natural and what seems easy. Who doesn't love to check things off of their to-do list? Unfortunately, the things that entrepreneurs are checking off their lists too often make no appreciable difference in their business or in their lives.

What's the solution? Profit production fixes almost everything.

A lot of entrepreneurs say to me, "I'm spending time on so many low-level tasks because I can't afford to get help." But the reason they can't afford the help is because they're not spending enough time on profit-producing activities.

When I started my business, I was working 60 hours a week as an executive. I had a team of 100 people. I was managing 17 locations that I had full responsibility for: budget, margins, metrics, sales. My job was 100% growth and leading sales teams. So when I started my business, before I even had a customer, the very first thing I did was hire an intern to support me with all the nonessential, tactical, administrative and operational tasks. I focused 100% of my time on three things and three things only:

1) Creating content, because I know that's how you generate leads and build an audience;
2) Having conversations, which is how you engage and nurture people; and
3) Having sales conversations.

This, in turn, led to a fourth activity, which I did in the evenings after putting my daughter Madison to bed: serving clients. That single-mindedness allowed my business to grow faster and defy the odds even though I had far fewer hours than the average business owner had to dedicate to building the business.

When I was starting out, I did what every good new entrepreneur does: I joined a coaching program — and I did so before I ever even had a customer. Why? I had business acumen but *zero* experience in the world of online business. When I started the coaching program, I was pumped and could not wait to watch my business explode before my eyes. But once I got into the program, I noticed myself feeling down, often comparing myself to others who were further along or spending more time on their businesses than I could. I found myself thinking, *I'm working so hard, and I'm never going to catch up. How am I ever going to get to a point where I can go full time with this?* That first year, I was like "the little engine that could." I was just getting started, putting the fundamentals in place. And, though I was seeing some traction, the beginning was slow.

Still, I signed up for a second year of the coaching program. This is when my business *really* started to take off. Here I was, surrounded by many of the same people who were with me in year one, and suddenly my business was growing and growing and *growing*. Meanwhile, those same people I was once comparing myself to were showing up to the coaching calls week after week, asking the same questions, stuck in the same place, struggling with the same problems.

This is when the light bulb went off.

It's not about how many hours per week you work. It's the focus and intent of those hours. Are you doing the right things with the hours that you *do* have?

> *"As a productivity coach and someone with ADHD, I am always looking for ways to simplify tasks. The Miracle Hour is a great example of not trying to do more but doing the right things in the time we have. It's not about efficiency so much as it is about effectiveness. It prioritizes revenue producing activities. Genius!"*
>
> *-Cindy Baker Coaching*

I am writing this book because far too many entrepreneurs sacrifice years of their life for "future" success just to find they gave up the most precious years of their lives. And I don't want that for you. Many small business owners are already putting in long hours but often not for the right things. They sacrifice their time with their children, they give up their health, they lose every part of themselves while chasing success that will forever be out of reach if they continue to do what they've always done. If the number of hours you worked determined success, we would have an overwhelming number of eight- and nine-figure entrepreneurs, but that is simply not the case.

My goal is to get people to spend at least one hour each day doing the right things. Because, for me, that one hour a day was completely life-changing.

My hope is to help you spend your time doing the right things in your business so that you can devote more time to meaningful pursuits in your actual day-to-day life. For me, that means homeschooling my daughter, working out with a personal trainer, being active in my local community, going to church, investing in my marriage and taking dance classes with friends. Today, I have time in my life for what matters because I focus my time and energy on the things that move the needle.

Breaking Free from Mindset Traps
Entrepreneurs may seem superhuman, but they fall prey to the same mindset traps as anyone else. Whether those traps involve failure or money, they often get passed down through generations. Growing up without strong financial role models, I didn't learn good habits, mindset or strategy until later in life.

I grew up in a very loving household, but my mom stayed at home to care for five children while my dad worked for a religious nonprofit. The salary he earned was not enough to support a family of seven. His false belief was that you can't both make money *and* do good.

I decided that I wanted my life to be very different from my father's from a young age. So I cleaned my dance studio in order to pay for classes, had five jobs while in college and prioritized financial freedom over everything else in my early career. I did all this just to escape the financial situation I was raised in.

> *"I've signed one new trust-building offer client, one signature program client and one upgrade with an existing client – total $6K!*
>
> *Learned so much from you."*
>
> *-Anonymous Virtual Business School Member*

It took me years to learn how to truly have it all, and this began with a mindset shift that translated into changing how I managed my time. If you want to be a successful entrepreneur and make *real* money, you have to focus your time and energy on the right things in your business. For me, that meant actively upgrading my mindset about money. I had to take on a new belief system: I *can* make millions and do good. I *can* change people's lives every single day, and I *can* build a successful, multimillion-dollar business. When I became the embodiment of this mentality, my life, results and impact exploded.

Maybe you're reading this and realizing that your money mindset could use an upgrade, too. The way to assess this is by reflecting on your own behavior. Are you spending your time on the things that will make your dream a reality? Or are you putting out fires, distracted by urgent but non-important tasks that make no real material difference in your life?

Faith and conviction are two sides of the same coin. Faith is belief in something you can't see. Conviction is the depth of certainty about what you have faith in. Know that God has great plans for you and you are just getting started, but you have to show up fully in order to receive the miracles He is waiting for you to be ready for. If you don't show up and sell with full conviction each day, how can you possibly make the impact or income that you desire?

It is important as a leader, business owner or entrepreneur to understand that there is a direct correlation between your beliefs about sales, money and success. Many leaders believe they can be hands-off with sales and still achieve high levels of success. But sales are where the transfer of inspiration happens. It is only when you truly show up as a leader with conviction around what you are selling, that you will be able to have the height of success that you desire both financially and from an impact standpoint.

One hour a day of focus can unlock dreams you prayed for, goals that seemed out of reach and success beyond imagination. This is your nudge to step into the arena.

Many business leaders want a dream team of their own that will make millions for their company, and this is fully available and possible for you. I have done it in my own company and helped many others do the same. However, you have to first commit to showing up, leading and getting down in the trenches in order to create the pathway to success for your team. I constantly hear from frustrated leaders that their team is not selling or performing, but when I ask a few questions about their involvement, it's either nonexistent or not supportive of what they are asking their team to achieve. As leaders, we go first. We pave the path to success, and only then can we pass the baton.

People tend to avoid sales because they don't want to be rejected. We fear failure. Our entire lives, we're taught that failure is bad. And yet, ironically, building a positive relationship with failure is required if you want to be a successful entrepreneur. Being an entrepreneur involves nothing if not trial and error: testing new strategies, identifying what works and what doesn't work, extracting lessons and applying those to future endeavors. The vast majority of entrepreneurs avoid making choices that are uncomfortable, steering clear of risks that could result in failure because of past programming from school and family systems. Nothing could be *less* productive.

Today, I challenge to you run full-force toward your dreams, and this means being willing to get in the trenches and connect with people daily (and with conviction). Inspire people to change their lives, follow your lead and take action to invest in you simply because they see the depth of your conviction. That will transform their confidence and belief that results are entirely possible for them. Sales are win-win. When you reframe your mindset around that, everything changes.

Reclaiming Your Time to Grow Your Income
By now, I hope you're getting excited and imagining what's possible for your business and life when you adopt an organized system like the Miracle Hour. Now, consider a vision you created way back when but stopped looking at because your goals felt out of reach. Revisit the dreams that you are not willing to let die. What are the top five dreams you will use the Miracle Hour to bring to life? List them on the following page.

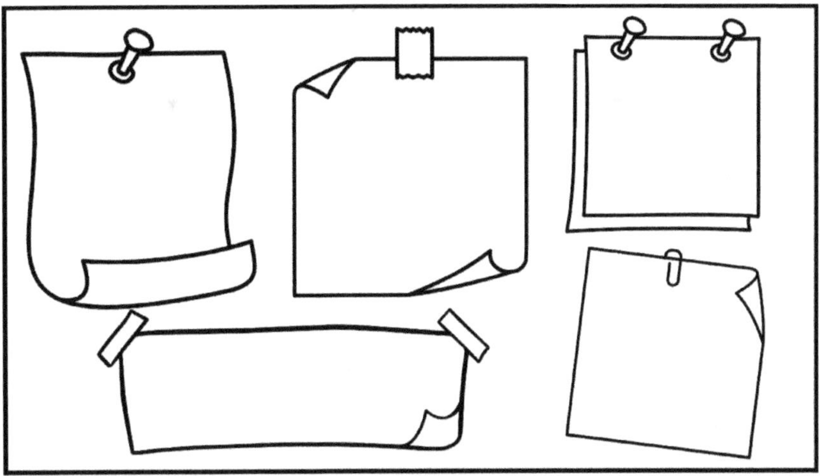

Now, let's answer the question, "Where do I begin?" It all starts with one hour a day — the Miracle Hour. I often joke that the Miracle Hour is called the Miracle Hour not because it is itself miraculous, but because it's miraculous if entrepreneurs do it. It doesn't take talent or skill; it takes commitment and conviction around living out your most sacred goals and dreams. For many business owners, the fear of missing out constantly pulls them out of deep, focused work and into scattered pursuits of success.

Studies show that one hour of deep work is equivalent to eight hours of distracted work. You do the math on how radically your life is about to change as a result of one focused hour.

At its basis, this strategy is so wildly simple that I taught my eleven-year-old daughter how to apply it. She and I run a club for girls ages seven to 14 called the Courage Club for which Madison runs her own Miracle Hour. The other day, I was sitting in a business meeting, and she was working three feet away from me, following her Miracle Hour for the Courage Club. Mid-hour, she got two *yeses* on the spot.

I know so many entrepreneurs who go into debt pursuing growth. Sometimes that's financial debt, but just as often it's emotional and spiritual debt; they compromise so many other areas of their life. Yet, when they lock into the right profit-producing activities, it doesn't take talent, money, a network or built-in advantages. It takes discipline and focus on the right things to get to their goals.

No matter where you are, you can start now. You can take back your focus and reclaim your power, starting today.

Deciding to Begin

I get it. Perhaps you've read other self-help books, tried other coaching programs, invested in your hopes and dreams only to discover that the unbelievable promise of simplicity was indeed just that: unbelievable. Allow me, then, to introduce the Magic Index Card.

I created the Magic Index Card back in the earliest days of building my business. At that point, I had a scant 60 minutes each day to devote to growing my business as I was still working full time. I literally took an index card and wrote down a list of what I could manage to get done in short bursts of time.

What could I do with 30 minutes?

What could I do with 15 minutes?

What could I do with 10 minutes, five minutes or even one minute to grow my business?

I knew the odds were stacked against me — namely, I did not have time. Beyond the 60 hours a week that I spent in the office, I had a newborn who required the around-the-clock care that newborns do. Instead of feeling demoralized, I looked for ways to *find* time. I knew I couldn't afford to be precious. That's why I broke it down into simple, actionable tasks and carried that card with me everywhere I went. Suddenly, my days were filled with opportunity in the form of five- and 10-minute-sized tasks. That's how I built a seven-figure business, which allowed me to replace my executive income before I could leave. All thanks to the Magic Index Card.

1-10 minutes
Post on social (feed + story)
Record a 1 minute tip
Send invites to book a call
Welcome messages to new followers
Engage on 5 people's content that you want to build relationships or work with
Sweep DM inbox
10-20 minutes
Post on social + record 5 stories/social clips
Follow up with consults/pending closes
Sweep post comments
Follow up with consults pending to close
Send invites to book call to upsell or add on
Send a follow up text/DM to 10 prospects you want to work with

Reach out to 5 past or ideal referral partners to invite them to share an upcoming series, workshop or launch
20-30 minutes
Go live
Record a podcast
Write and send an email to your list
Schedule a consultation
Send 30 prospect follow ups
Record 15 2-minute videos for social
Record 15 stories for social
Inbox sweep to invite to next steps or share a value-add resource
Folllow up block to invite to consults/follow up on past consults
Reach out to 10 people or ask for referrals
Welcome messages to new followers + thread/DM sweeps

During one of our homeschooling days together, I actually helped my daughter create her first Magic Index Card. Madison, like so many kids, is *busy*. She is a full-time homeschool student (my husband, Billy, teaches her the traditional subjects while I focus on investing, public speaking, sales, marketing, business, personal development and Christianity). She's also a competitive dancer, so almost every night of the week and on the weekends she's in rehearsals with her team. And she often spends time with friends and family on the weekend when she is not at the studio.

As we were working together to grow the Courage Club and discussing her goals, she told me that her goal was to reach 400 members by the end of the year. I explained to her that the way she was going to make that happen was by implementing the Miracle Hour and creating an index card of her own to follow.

In these pages, I'll teach you how to create your own Magic Index Card and implement your own Miracle Hour. But in return, you have to make the decision to prioritize making your dreams come true. Staying comfortable with the status quo isn't going to move the needle. You have to commit to change. Before we get started, answer the questions on the following pages.

Where have you allowed yourself to get comfortable by staying stuck?

____

____

____

Where do you need to direct your focus and attention to achieve the life you deserve and desire?

____

____

____

If you close your eyes for a moment and fast-forward a year into the future, what is the number one thing you want to achieve in your business or life?

____

____

____

How will you enter the arena and take action?

____

____

____

____

      Finally, what action items will this require of you on a daily basis when you have an extra minute or 30 minutes? Whether it's committing to consistent posting, reaching out personally to new followers, engaging with prospects or going live to your community, think about all of the direct actions that will yield meaningful results. Take a minute to fill out your own Magic Index Card.

The Magic Index Card is the foundation of your Miracle Hour activities. It's not about revolutionary tactics. It's about being disciplined enough to commit to daily, consistent actions.

There came a point during my executive career when I had to decide to be more connected to the future than to the past. If I wanted something, I had to commit to taking action even if it meant doing so imperfectly (and refining as I went). It's like that idiom, where there's a will, there's a way. Whether you're in a career and have a dream of starting your own business one day, or you have a business and are ready to take a new direction or reach a new level, this can work for you.

Every dream that comes true begins with the decision to commit to a plan. If you're someone who struggles with commitment, follow-through, accountability and implementation, I invite you to visit https://www.thekellyroach.com/miracle and download your free Miracle Hour toolkit. This will equip you with the exact framework, structure and templates required to win with the Miracle Hour. I also support clients as they implement their own Miracle Hour with my Virtual Business School program, which includes on-demand trainings and templates, live hot-seat coaching three times per month, live implementation support and monthly marketing masterclasses. If you are interested in joining a community of online service providers who are focused on growth and mastering predictable daily sales, visit https://www.virtualbusinessschool.com.

Chapter 2: Reclaiming Control, One Hour at a Time

A year and a half ago, I woke up, stood in front of the mirror and realized that I didn't recognize the person looking back at me. Long before I climbed the corporate ladder, I was an NFL cheerleader. For nearly my whole life, I'd been a competitive dancer. I was used to being fit, strong, muscular. Yet there I was, 41 years old, staring in the mirror, wondering: Who *is* this person?

After two decades in the working world, dedicating my time and energy to business and family, my health had taken a back seat. Clearly, ignoring wellness had come with visible costs. Realizing that I'd let my health slip from the top of my priorities troubled me. It wasn't just a matter of toning up or losing weight; I wanted to feel better, to be confident in my own skin again. It was time to get my body back, so I embarked on a health journey.

Approaching this new venture, the business of my wellness, I knew I had to be thoughtful. As a busy working mom, helming six companies with a family and home (while also homeschooling my daughter), I couldn't afford to drop everything and devote hours to the gym, prepping food and counting calories and macros. I had to reclaim my body in a way that complemented the rest of my life. I asked myself, *What can I do that's sustainable, that will accommodate my schedule?* After trying a few different trainers, I found Amanda Ferreira and started working out with her virtually three to four times a week for 30 minutes.

Within months, I saw the results compounding: I'd lost almost 20 pounds, gained muscle, dropped two sizes and massively increased my confidence. Not only did my energy explode, but my relationships improved. I actually began to enjoy shopping again — just a little bit — because everything fit with ease, and I was saving so much time not having to try on 10 different outfits to find something I felt confident wearing.

This is the power of the Miracle Hour in any form or facet. What was truly surprising was that I hadn't even dedicated a full hour a day to my health and fitness — it was only about 90 minutes per *week*. I got the right coach, focused on the right things for me and did them with consistency, frequently.

The takeaway? What we focus on is what gets done. Where we put our energy is where we'll see outcomes.

Although I'm a business growth strategist and I teach the Miracle Hour in a sales context, this practice can be applied to *any* area of life you want to transform. Whether it's improving your marriage or your relationship with your children, changing careers, starting a new hobby, mastering an instrument or getting your health in order, if you dedicate an hour a day to it, there's no way you won't see massive results.

Yes, the Miracle Hour is a daily sales system that will produce income and profits in your business every single day. But I would challenge you to look at the other areas of your life that could benefit from it. And remember: No area is off limits.

Here's another example: For many years, I've been a person of faith. I grew up in a faith-centered family. Throughout the course of my life, I zigged and zagged and had to find my own individual and direct relationship with God. My faith has been my secret weapon in business and life. When I went through some of the worst rock-bottom seasons of my life, it was my faith that got me through. After 10 years of being a business growth strategist, focusing primarily on sales, marketing, operational effectiveness and team building, I realized I could no longer attribute my success to strategy and hard work, but instead to the gifts and glory of God. I knew God was calling me to go deeper to share my faith — not just strategy — and to invite leaders to invite God into their lives and businesses in a more meaningful way.

As I began the pursuit of sharing my faith in my work and life publicly, I quickly found I didn't have the words to articulate what I was trying to convey. I felt ill-equipped and elementary in my faith. It was time to commit to growth. I decided that every morning, I'd spend the first thirty minutes of the day listening to the Bible and praying. I replaced reading one business book a week with a spiritual or faith-related one.

Guess what? My faith grew. The depth of my spiritual life, happiness, gratitude and perspective expanded exponentially. I know I still have many years of work to do in order to share my faith more eloquently, but I try and I am continuing to improve.

Here is what encourages me: Over the last year, countless people have come to me and shared sentiments like, "You sharing your faith brought me back to mine." Students, clients and peers have told me that because of what I've shared, they got their first Bible, returned to church and even found God again.

I share this because absolutely everything we do has an incredible ripple effect in the world. When you grow, the byproduct is that everyone around you is impacted. When you commit to the Miracle Hour, whether for your finances, faith, fitness, fulfillment or relationships, you will transform and the world around you will benefit as a result.

The world produces countless distractions that deter us from our dreams and goals. When we spend our time fending off distractions — let alone reacting or responding to them — we can start to feel like nothing we do matters. Like we're powerless. But I believe that a state of powerlessness is not a foregone conclusion. This book is a rallying cry against those forces that hold us back and bring us down.

Do you have a free hour today? If so, it's time to take back your life. If you answered no, it's time to re-evaluate your time, priorities and focus to uncover your Miracle Hour.

Take a few minutes now to audit your calendar. Before we get into *what*, let's start with *when*. If you are serious about achieving an audacious, God-sized goal, you have to start by finding the time to make it a reality. None of us *have* the time; we *find* the time. I recommend that your Miracle Hour be the same time every day so that you can create a consistent cadence and habit around the daily actions that must happen. The path to compressing a 10-year goal into six months or less comes down to:

1) Frequency — how often you execute;
2) Consistency — steadiness and regularity of your execution; and
3) Quality — effectiveness of your execution.

In order to have the bandwidth to increase your frequency, consistency and quality of execution, begin by identifying what you will cut or eliminate from your calendar.

What needs to be eliminated to make space for your Miracle Hour (delegate, outsource or delete all together)?

____

____

____

____

____

____

____

____

____

____

____

Now, commit! When will your Miracle Hour take place each day? Circle it, highlight it, add a star next to it. This hour *officially* now belongs to making your dreams come true.

WHEN WILL YOUR MIRACLE HOUR TAKE PLACE EACH DAY?

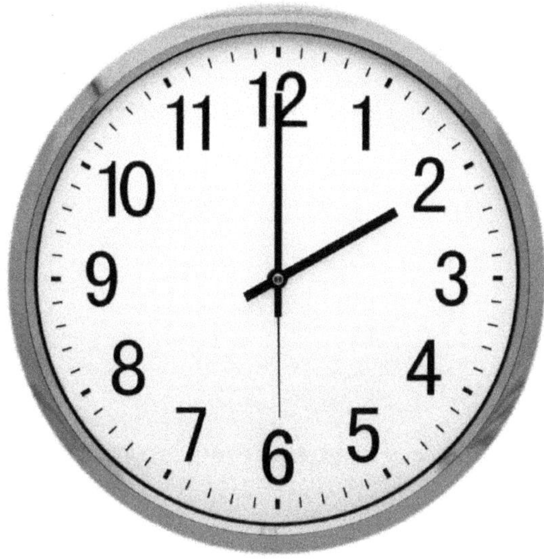

Keep in mind that the less task switching, changing and rearranging you do, the more likely this hour will happen. Come to your Miracle Hour prepared with everything that you need to be successful. For example, if you plan on reaching out to past clients to reignite the conversation, come with a list ready. You don't need complex technology or automations. If you're an early-stage entrepreneur, you don't even need a customer relationship management system (CRM), you can use a spreadsheet. Keep it simple, and don't wait for the perfect "timing" to get started.

> *"Just wanted to say how good it felt to be so productive in an hour. Doing the Miracle Hour together today was FUN. This is EXACTLY what I needed. Starting Miracle Hour #2 for the day, because, why not?"*
>
> *-Anonymous Virtual Business School Member*

Defining Your Impact Areas and Overcoming "Calling Confusion"

As I look at my life today, everything Billy and I dreamed of 20 years ago has come to fruition. We live a true faith- and family-first life. We have time freedom, location freedom and decision freedom. We were able to take full ownership of Madison's education and homeschool together. We are actively involved in our church and local community, focus on our health and fitness daily and have been able to relocate from Pennsylvania to our dream home in Florida (a place we used to vacation). Our lives are our own, and that means we get to be all-in parents and donate money and resources to important causes. I have the autonomy to retire when I choose (although I have no desire to do this since my work is a calling, not a career).

Sacrifice, teamwork, prayer and intentional action will do this in your life. I truly believe that you can have it all, but to have it all, you need discipline and intention. You need to know what you really want.

The true essence of the Miracle Hour is a simple daily sales system: one hour a day dedicated to profit-producing activities that will grow your business. But unsurprisingly, those activities will vary from person to person, role to role and company to company.

How do you determine what should happen in that hour? We start by reverse-engineering your goals. Your Miracle Hour, your daily sales system, starts with you defining what success means for you.

Say you're an author. If you have a huge book launch coming up, your Miracle Hour might consist of pitching your book proposal. It may include reaching out to book PR and media appearances or contacting people who you want to send the book to and asking them to promote it online. It also may include building your promotional team and reaching out to peers, colleagues and influential contacts to share and promote your book during its launch week.

Using preparation for an upcoming book launch as an example, your Miracle Hour could consist of the following impact areas:

1) Reaching out to secure PR appearances and podcast interviews to promote the book;
2) Pitching agents to get a book deal;
3) Reaching out to build your street team to promote the book;
4) Sending direct messages, emails and texts to invite relevant parties to prelaunch or preorder activities to drive preorders; and
5) Booking virtual or in-person speaking appearances to sell bulk orders and promote the book.

If you are a business coach selling products, programs or services online, it might look like:

1) Posting on social media daily, rotating between value-add content, promoting an opt-in or lead magnet to build your list, or promoting your offers;
2) Sending a sales text message or email to your contact list;
3) Going live once a week to drive sales while spending the rest of the week following up with attendees and registrants;
4) Sending follow-ups to warm leads who haven't closed;
5) Engaging with past customers to build rapport and reactivate;
6) Engaging with your top prospects on their content to add value for them; and
7) Booking 15-minute calls to connect and qualify leads, or 30-minute consultations with qualified leads to close.

This is what I call *defining your impact areas*. Impact areas are activities you'll commit to no matter what, every single day, in a set quantity. It's a systematic approach to success — no wishing or hoping required.

Why does this matter for you? Because billion-dollar corporations operate based on systems. They operate based on KPIs and metrics. Those corporations determine the outcome they want and the input required to achieve that outcome. The Miracle Hour makes success systematic, repeatable and scalable.

What continues to shock me about the entrepreneurial world is that small businesses don't run their businesses like businesses. Most entrepreneurs wake up in the morning and puzzle over what to do that day. They question what they'll focus on and how they'll make a sale or get a result. There's no plan, no process. Unsurprisingly, the business is chaotic. Since the business is their life, it stands to reason that their life is chaotic, too.

The Miracle Hour starts with defining your goal. This is a crucial part of the process.

For over a decade, I've unfortunately witnessed far too many entrepreneurs building businesses that they're not passionate about — businesses they don't even like. These entrepreneurs don't enjoy running their businesses because they're not pursuing their goals. They're pursuing their mentors' goals or the goals of someone they follow on Instagram. All of a sudden, they're committing time, energy and financial resources to creating and replicating something that is not God's design for them. That's why it's so important to factor reflection time into your Miracle Hour, especially when you're getting started.

Where do you feel you are being called in your business to use your unique gifts to be of service?

____

____

____

____

Does your business in its current form support this?

____

____

____

____

What (if any) changes do you need to make to create alignment with this?

____

____

____

____

What are the top three goals for your business this year?

1: ____

2: ____

3: ____

What are the top impact areas that you know will move the needle on these goals?

1: ____

2: ____

3: ____

4: ____

5: ____

6: ____

7: ____

Where do you personally need to be putting your energy and focus in order for this to happen?

____

____

____

We have all been given spiritual gifts, this perfect design that God has imprinted upon each of us. The Miracle Hour can help you realize that design. But to do so, you'll have to ensure what you are building and moving toward is a goal that is *yours* and yours *alone*.

You'll have to listen to hear what you've been called to do.

Easier said than done — I get it. As I mentioned, I've worked with countless entrepreneurs who have no idea what they want to create. Why is it so difficult to know what we want? Why is it that the average business owner can't even spend one hour a day on productive activity? One cause is surely our level of distraction.

Take, for example, social media. Either you work for social media or it works for you. Most leaders are slowly letting their dreams slip away because scrolling, comparison and consumption take their most precious, unrecoverable asset: their time. Make social media instead work for you. It is your microphone to the world. If you are on it, use that time to post, livestream or interact directly with your audience instead of passively consuming. Do not let it steal your dream and your focus.

When you spend more time consuming than creating, you are being influenced subconsciously in a multitude of ways. For many entrepreneurs, this shows up like pursuing goals that they're ill-suited for. This is why I believe that being self-led and having a prayer life are so important. If you're accustomed to reflection and inward contemplation, your values and priorities will dictate the decisions that you're making, what you're pursuing, and who you're becoming. The Miracle Hour should be the vehicle that takes you to that destination that's right *for you*. Often that means having courage and following a different path than the people around you.

Many entrepreneurs struggle with this. And yet, given that we're frequently the first in our families or peer groups to reach a certain milestone, we must become comfortable breaking out of the pack and saying, "No, I'm going this way instead." I had to do just that many years ago as an entrepreneur. I saw how people were acting online with the rise of social media — chasing clicks, striving to entertain versus add real value and flexing lifestyle over building an actual life they're proud of.

This is exactly why I wrote my book *Conviction Marketing*. I wanted to show entrepreneurs that they can be true to themselves without succumbing to the latest online trends. That they can instead focus on authenticity, integrity, adding value and building wildly successful brands without chasing fads or virality. Most entrepreneurs simply react and respond, mimicking what others do online. Ironically, the vast majority of people they're observing aren't even successful; it's a smoke and mirrors effect. It's a waste of time and energy when an entrepreneur blindly replicates something that someone else is doing, especially when on the inside, that person isn't even experiencing the level of success they portray.

Grab your copy of Conviction Marketing

That's why the Miracle Hour is so crucial. Not only does it give you a system for daily sales, but it also allows you to reclaim control of the direction of your business and life.

Miracle Hour Execution

The Miracle Hour starts with three steps:

Step One: Define Your Outcome

Example: *I want to make at least one sale a day as a direct result of my Miracle Hour activities.*

Write down your desired outcome here:

____

____

____

____

____

Step Two: Decide Which Activities to Repeat Daily to Reach to Your Goals

Identify which activities have the highest likelihood of getting you to your goals. I recommend naming five to seven core activities that will get you to your desired outcome.

Pro tip: Use the 80/20 rule. Typically, the majority (80%) of results come from a small fraction (20%) of effort. Do referrals drive the majority of your client acquisitions? If so, prioritize asking happy clients for introductions. Have most of your sales come from live launches and masterclasses? Get more live sessions on the calendar. Make sure your top historic success mechanisms are your key focus areas, but with expanded intent and volume.

Example: If you're an online entrepreneur and you want to make daily sales on social media, some of your activities might include posting in your Facebook group, posting a story with a strategic call to action or following up on past threads with people who have expressed interest in a specific topic. Identify the activities that will make the greatest impact in relation to your goals. (Reminder: These should coincide with the activities on your Magic Index Card).

1: ____

2: ____

3: ____

4: ____

5: ____

6: ____

7: ____

Step Three: Determine the quantity of actions you need to complete at minimum each day or week in order to achieve the outcome you identified above.

Assign a starting quantity to each impact action on the following sheet. You will not know that exact number right away, and that's OK. Start by setting a baseline, then measure and track against that number. Refine as you go. Don't overthink it— define, test, iterate.

Example: If the activity is reaching out to clients and colleagues for referrals, the goal might be reaching out to five people per day.

MY MIRACLE HOUR ACTIVITIES:

ACTIVITY	GOAL

Let's Recap

So far, we have discussed:

1) A set time your Miracle Hour will happen each day;
2) Your Miracle Hour goal;
3) Your five to seven impact areas; and
4) The quantity of each daily activity.

Over the course of the following chapters, we'll delve into the steps of Miracle Hour even further. But before we do, a word of caution: I often remind my clients that eight-figure entrepreneurs are the ones who obsess over the basic fundamentals that six-figure entrepreneurs consider themselves "too advanced" for.

Let that sink in.

As someone who has built an eight-figure company and helped many others do the same, please understand you are never going to advance out of the fundamentals of growth. In fact, one of the reasons many entrepreneurs never advance from six to eight figures is that they don't want to get their hands dirty with the essentials of what actually drives growth. On the other hand, those who do see scalable growth are *obsessed* with getting the basics working well and then scaling exponentially.

Growth does not have to be complex or revolutionary. Often, it's spending time on those simple fundamentals that are what drive the biggest results. It starts with cultivating the right habits and having discipline to execute them every single day—without distraction or excuses.

Make Daily Offers (And Other Seven- and Eight-Figure Activities)

Eight-figure leaders don't run their businesses on "vibes" and emotions. They run on systems and strategies that take into consideration buyer mentality and consumer behavior. Let's take a look at the reality of how sales work:

1) A ZipDo report from 2026 shows that modern buyers consume around 12-13 pieces of content before engaging with sales or making a purchase decision;
2) Forty-seven percent of buyers will view three to five pieces of content before ever talking to a sales rep; and
3) Buyers often complete 60-70% of their decision-making process before talking to sales.

A 2026 data report by WifiTalents shows that up to 80% of sales require five or more follow-ups after the initial contact, and a typical sale isn't closed until five to seven deliberate touches have been made.

Now, I want to ask you, which of these buyer stats is your sales system built around? Is your sales system built to capitalize on buying behavior or fight against it? The reality of doing business online is that millions of dollars of revenue sit in our inboxes at any given time. I hear from business owners constantly that they just "need more leads." Yet, 85% of sales happen in the eighth to 12th follow-up. That means the average entrepreneur — the entrepreneur who *doesn't* follow up more than once — is leaving over 85% of sales on the table.

Even worse, they're losing opportunities with people who have already expressed interest in some way, shape or form. Think about all the money you've likely left on the table as a result of workshop registrations that didn't convert, consults that didn't convert, lead magnet opt-ins that were never personally followed up with.

This is why eight-figure businesses are so rare (and why the average business owner takes home $50,000 or less). The vast majority of people never follow up after the first or second point of contact, when all the business is being done in follow-ups nine to 12.

The Miracle Hour is about stopping this obsessive focus on "more." So many entrepreneurs get taken out of the game because they burn out before they ever scale up. The chase for *more* is exhausting. But what if instead you focused on high-intent, quality relationships that converted into high paying clients predictably and consistently?

Get off that nonstop hamster wheel of *more* and instead focus on building relationships. Connect with people who have expressed interest in your product, service or program and invite them to take action. This is where the magic happens.

Shockingly, if I were to survey 1,000 entrepreneurs and ask how many of them actually made offers to their market every single day, it would probably be less than 1%. While everyone wants to make sales every day, no one is actually inviting people to work with them. How entitled are we to think that people will show up for a party that we never invited them to? Where did this mindset come from?

In the hustle and grind of the Fortune 500 world, before we had social media at our fingertips 24-7, there was none of that. We made dozens of cold calls each day. We were out in front of businesses prospecting daily — yes, in person. We didn't wait for business to materialize out of nowhere. How lucky are we that in the business climate of today, we never have to make a cold call or pitch ever again? There are plenty of opportunities right in our own ecosystems online. We just have to work them.

If you want people to want to work with you, you have to *invite them* to work with you.

The Miracle Hour teaches entrepreneurs, among other things, the power of making offers. When I look at my daughter's

Miracle Hour success with making offers, those sales came from leads who expressed interest that she simply followed up with.

> *"My team has generated $150K in licensing deals using Miracle Hour (on) LinkedIn exclusively."*
>
> *-Maria Fontana, Founder at Maria Fontana Consulting*

Making offers, making invitations, going live, doing the fundamentals — that's how easy the Miracle Hour is. But, as I said, the entrepreneurs still struggling to reach seven or eight figures think these fundamentals are too basic for them. They want more. However, it's these fundamentals that drive a business forward. It's simple: Input creates output.

If you want to take your business seriously (and the Miracle Hour is about taking your business seriously), you can't approach each day disorganized, wishing and hoping, and taking random action that you hope leads to outcome. Instead, you (and everyone on your team) need a clear, repeatable system. Get clear on the outcome, determine what the input looks like and what categories it will consist of, and decide the quantity of that input.

Once you've achieved a cadence for doing the right activities in the right quantity then you can focus on the *effectiveness* of those activities to increase output. This refinement is how you grow from one sale a day to two sales a day, then double, triple, quadruple results from there. I started this process at zero, just like everyone else. Now it's snowballed into hundreds of sales per month.

In fact, I'd bet that you could stop reading for a few minutes right now and take action on your activities to generate a dream client. Think about it: It takes less than one minute to send a message to a prospect. Ask yourself what "open loop" opportunities exist in your business right now that you can follow up on. Can you identify five people you spoke to in the past who expressed interest but didn't commit? Can you follow up with them right now? Who are your best referral partners? Reach out to them and see who they have come across recently who would benefit from your services. Can you reach out to a past customer who took a break but who you think may be ready to pick back up?

We did this exercise in person at one of my events recently, and a client of mine generated a $30,000 sale on the spot! See how simple it can be? It's all about focus, energy and intent. You can send that message in 60 seconds or less and generate thousands of dollars for your business.

How many people in your audience do you connect with each day? What should that number be in order to achieve your goals? Start today. Start now.

Overcoming the "Sales" Stigma

Many people, including entrepreneurs, find themselves bothered by the very idea of sales. Most elite entrepreneurs do not believe they have any mindset issues around sales until we dig into what they want to achieve and measure that against what they are doing to achieve that result. We can say, "I don't mind selling" or "I'm pretty good at sales" but then simultaneously keep ourselves busy doing everything but sales. Then we feel distraught when the company underperforms.

The same leaders who don't sell themselves are frustrated and disappointed when their team is not selling consistently or successfully. You are the role model for your team, your clients and the market. If it's crucial to the success of the company model, lead the way and show your team what success looks like. Give them something to replicate and aspire to. That is real leadership.

In my forthcoming book, *The Sacred Art of Selling*, I advocate viewing yourself as a steward who champions other people's success. If you're passionate about your product, your service, your solution, but you're not passionate enough to reach out to people to share your offering, you might need to reconsider your conviction about helping people.

Today, many people in the business world hide behind the notion of service. "I just want to help people," they protest, explaining why they don't sell. Unfortunately, it's difficult to help people if you don't sell anything. Investment precedes transformation, commitment triggers change. If you want people to benefit from your product, program or service, and get the best results, those people need to invest.

One of the reasons I love teaching sales is because I get to empower people like you to impact thousands of lives for good. When you follow a daily sales system you can do this predictably with frameworks, open-ended questions and strategic invitations that feel good for everyone involved. When you have a true sales system you do not need to resort to tactics or strategies that remove the integrity from what the core of a service-based business is all about: service.

At the end of the day, you need to *believe* in the value you're bringing. When someone interacts with you, they should trust that you're committed to your business and the transformation it will provide for people. When you're not confident around sales, people aren't confident about investing in you.

Yes, sales may have been taught unscrupulously in the past. Plenty of people have had a negative sales experience, and they are now resistant to it. But as many before me have said: Be the change you want to see in the world. If you had a negative sales experience, change that outcome for someone. Reflect on the following:

What is the most positive sales experience you have experienced? Why?

____

____

____

What were some of the negative sales experiences you have had? Why?

____

____

____

What would reflect the best experience you have had? What would be the opposite of the negative experience you have had? Define the characteristics of a *positive* sales experience.

____

____

____

With this exercise, you'll define your signature sales style — one that allows you to show up in an authentic, meaningful, high-integrity way that will get you to the desired outcome and allow you to feel amazing in the process.

Your Next Million-Dollar Breakthrough
With social media, we have people entering our world every day from so many directions that most businesses have the *opposite* problem of needing more exposure. Entrepreneurs are not actually covering existing leads with a clear system for nurturing consistent follow-ups. Yet, they still wake up and chase new leads instead of slowing down and investing in connecting and building relationships with the people right in front of them.

In my Virtual Business School program, we teach a relationship-management process that makes it incredibly simple and straightforward to manage the leads who already exist in your ecosystem. Pair an organized framework with your Miracle Hour activities, and you're off to the races. If you're curious about working with my team to create sale predictability and a simple daily cadence for results that compound, you can visit https://www.virtualbusinessschool.com. The only thing standing in the way of your next million-dollar breakthrough is you.

> *"I implemented the Miracle Hour, and secured a $30K client!*
>
> *-Anonymous Virtual Business School Member*

Despite the elimination of so many hurdles online, many people are still averse to following up with the people in closest proximity to them who are most likely to buy. Follow-up is a hallmark of the Miracle Hour. Let me repeat: Most sales happen between the ninth and 12th touchpoint. Without a system for follow-up and a process where you dedicate time every day to moving people to the next stage of the buying process, you're limited to a sliver of the sales that happen at the top of the funnel. That won't build a successful business. This is why 85% of businesses fail — they rely on people selling themselves into their offers, which rarely happens.

Following up applies to your existing clients and customers as well, not just new leads. I learned this the hard way. As I was building my first business, we were growing so fast that we only focused on our primary product. We neglected to focus on continuity, add-ons and upsell offers. As a result, we weren't selling our existing customers other products and services. Inevitably, those customers started hiring other people and receiving conflicting advice. Being told to go in two different directions is a recipe for overwhelm and disaster. Soon, our customers saw the success and results that they'd achieved with us unraveling because now they were working with someone who didn't have the same philosophy or track record. That was painful.

My team and I witnessed people we'd helped build six- and seven-figure businesses listen to awful advice from other service providers and suffer the consequence. I knew this was my fault. We weren't making the right offers at the right time to our existing customers. You cannot be afraid to sell to the market or to your own customers. Many avoid this because they think their customers may dislike being solicited, but the reality is that they will either get additional help from you or from someone else.

Let's face it, it's terrible to see a valuable customer, someone who has so much potential, miss out because they decided to work with someone who will never be able to help them get there. It's terrible to see them disappointed, frustrated or worse, taken advantage of. Sadly, this is a common scenario. It's one of the reasons we started the Conviction Marketing Agency. We were tired of seeing people be taken advantage of and spending tens of thousands of dollars at agencies that wouldn't deliver on their promises. Sometimes, they wouldn't even complete the project.

Do you make consistent add-on and upsell offers to your customers? Do you see unmet needs that you could be supporting so that customers don't have to go elsewhere for support? What action can you take on this today?

Bulletproofing Your Business — and Your Mindset

Without realizing it, entrepreneurs routinely self-sabotage. They do so by giving away their time to things that do not contribute to servicing their existing clients or getting new ones. Over time, the business takes over their lives, requiring more and more time, energy and money just to keep it afloat because they are simply not doing direct, high-impact activities. Entrepreneurs waste so much time tinkering with websites that potential clients won't even see rather than actually building their audience and having conversations with the market. That all changes with the Miracle Hour.

My passion for sales stems from the fact that I believe each of us are here for a reason. In my heart of hearts, I believe God made each of us to be of service and meaningfully contribute to the world. If you're an entrepreneur, you believe that your gift is to serve others. Guess what? Sales is the fundamental way that you will deploy that gift. There's no way around it. Entrepreneurs tell themselves stories about wanting to be of service, but at the end of the day, sales is your best methodology. If you want to be of service, you have to enroll people in the dream. Transformation requires investment and skin in the game. Your true path to changing the world and influencing others for good is through sales.

That is why we partner with CEOs and teams to master the systems around daily sales at the Virtual Business School. This includes optimizing their offer suite with "easy yes" offers to drive people into their ecosystem on the front end. We help them execute and master the Miracle Hour and continuously refine their Dream 1000. If you are interested in further accountability and support, visit https://www.virtualbusinessschool.com.

Don't forget to download your Miracle Hour toolkit to get started right away with templates, word tracks and a clear path to setting you and your team up for Miracle Hour success: https://www.thekellyroach.com/miracle.

Chapter 3: The Millionaire Mindset: Beliefs That Generate Millions

Like many entrepreneurs, I needed to learn how to build a business. Those learnings are what allowed me to expand and grow multiple six- and eight-figure companies. Today, I get to help thousands of people shortcut the learning curve, but I had to learn much of this through experience and years of trial and error. As a result, I have accumulated a set of beliefs around what it truly takes to win in business and in life, and I want to share them with you.

Belief #1: No One Needs to Lose in Order for You to Win
The biggest thing that I've learned on my entrepreneurial journey is that the more people you help, the more people you serve, the more people whose dreams you facilitate coming true, the easier it will be for you to succeed.

There are so many false constructs around money, many of which have been passed down through generations. Our projections of fear and scarcity make us believe that there's some limited quantity available to us, or that someone else has to lose in order for us to win, or that the only means to acquiring money is by acting without integrity. Maybe you grew up hearing your parents talking at the dinner table: "I wonder what they did to get that house" or "They must be doing something shady if they're able to go to Hawaii on spring break."

Like I said, growing up, my father worked for a religious nonprofit. He wanted to dedicate his life to service and to God, to doing good in the world. This was a beautiful aspiration. Yet my father had five children to support, and his choice of work meant that our family lived just above the poverty line. His belief that in order to do good, he could not make money had real repercussions. After standing in the free lunch line and receiving other forms of charity as a child, I've consciously worked to change that mindset in my adult life. I've had to say to myself, "I'm going to release that belief and adopt a new belief." We have the ability to both make money *and* do tremendous good in the world.

I've been able to support that belief over the course of building my business. We have funded multiple clean water projects with the nonprofit Charity: Water. This includes funding wells and water projects and providing clean drinking water to countries around the globe. I've been able to contribute to organizations that provide disaster relief, award scholarships to those who cannot afford our services but need a chance and fund church planting efforts to bring the Gospel to more people around the world. None of this would be possible without boldly selling our services with conviction each day. Building a successful, profitable business has funded my ability to give back in a meaningful way.

Today, in everything that I teach, in every book that I write, in every podcast that I record, in every company that I create and in every service that I deliver, my focus is on how I can help others win, which means I will too. By adopting the mindset that you can win by helping others win, you internalize the belief that the more people you help win, the more money you'll make. The ability to question beliefs that were instilled in us without our choice is a sign of maturity and growth.

What new beliefs are you ready to take on about what is possible in your life?

____

____

____

____

____

____

What are some things you want to do to be of service in the world as your business becomes more profitable and successful?

____

____

____

____

____

____

What are some beliefs about money that it's time to let go of?

____

____

____

____

____

Our lives are a self-fulfilling prophecy based on the choices we make. If you believe that money is bad or that you should feel shame for desiring to make millions of dollars, then either you will not make millions of dollars or you will and you'll lose it all. If instead you say, "I am a good steward. I invest, I save and I give back. I can earn millions of dollars, and I can do so with integrity while being of service to other people and making a meaningful, lasting difference in their lives," then you will create a radically different outcome for yourself. All of us have the power to choose.

Our world is rich in opportunities. We live in an incredible moment in time when it's more feasible than ever to use our platforms for good. We have so much power and influence to do good in the world, but doing good often requires resources. The success of my business determines my ability to give back in a meaningful way. When I donate to water projects through Charity: Water, that involves money. It costs money to build a well in a developing country where people don't have access to clean drinking water. When you make money, you put yourself in a position to meet the needs of others. After growing up as a recipient of aid, being on the other side of that equation is profoundly moving and empowering. It's an incredible feeling.

I'll reiterate: The millionaire mindset comes down to understanding that no one needs to lose in order for you to win. Mindset always precedes mechanics, which people rarely realize. That resistance to sales? It's because of your beliefs. Your hesitancy to pull in seven figures? Beliefs. Beliefs dictate mindset, and since mindset dictates behaviors, and behaviors dictate actions, *beliefs* determine the outcome of your life. If you change your belief, you change your mindset and you'll change your entire life.

Consider people who have done unbelievable things in the world: leaders, business icons, artists, humanitarians. These super-achieving people all have incredible stories about overcoming adversity and struggle. And yet, the reason those people have incredible stories to tell is because they didn't quit. They didn't quit *no matter what.* You'll never see a person who has a high level of success, or makes millions of dollars, who doesn't have stories about how they almost lost it all. How they almost gave up. How they endured horrible things. But they fought their battles and persevered because that's what they had to go through to achieve success. On the other hand, what stories do we hear about people who quit? Tales of obstacles, difficulty, long nights and, ultimately, backing down. Others endure all the same challenges except they decide to keep going. That's why mindset must come before mechanics. It's what you decide about your life.

Belief #2: You Are Responsible for Becoming the Person Your Dreams Require

The Miracle Hour is about putting a stake in the ground and saying, "I am willing to commit to becoming the person that my dreams require." That means going beyond merely *talking* about having a seven- or eight- or nine-figure business; it means, instead, *becoming* that seven- or eight- or nine-figure business owner by behaving accordingly. From your behavior to how you manage your calendar to the activities you're doing every day, all of it contributes to you becoming the person that your dreams require.

When I first began working with small business owners, I was shocked by the incongruence between people's stated goals and how they actually behaved. This is the reason I developed such a commitment to teaching sales and, frankly, writing books like this one. Entrepreneurs tell me they want one thing, but too often, when I examine what they are doing, there isn't alignment. If you say you want to make millions and make a difference in the world by providing scholarships or donating resources to people in need, yet you're not doing at least one hour a day of profit-producing activities to make the money to be able to do those things, there is misalignment.

Entrepreneurs frequently fall into the trap of buying into people who tell them they can skip over the steps required to make their dreams come true. That's why it's so crucial for entrepreneurs to be wildly discerning about who they listen to, who they study, who they watch, who they model themselves after, whose fingerprints they allow on their business. Plenty of people have made entire careers out of selling entrepreneurs shortcuts that will destroy their businesses and their lives. At the same time, if you're following someone with integrity, who's built something lasting and legitimate, that person will be honest about your responsibility to create congruence between what you say you want and the person you must become to make those dreams come true.

Let me be clear: Sometimes becoming the person that your dreams require involves making sacrifices. If, say, you want to earn more income, maybe that means working on Saturdays. If you want to advance to another level in your craft, that may mean taking night classes. Business aside, there is no person who performs at an elite level in any single area of life who is not doing extraordinary things and making the requisite sacrifices. Still, it's important to understand that making sacrifices doesn't mean sacrificing everything. For example, working a few hours on Saturday morning still leaves the rest of the weekend for working out, doing fun things with family, meeting up with friends, going out Saturday night, attending church on Sunday morning and more. This is how you cultivate the mindset of people who have built substantial, lasting businesses over decades.

The problem arises when we decide we want the outcome without putting in the work. Do you want to be a millionaire? If so, invest time in learning about money. Spend your money on assets, not on things that are depreciating liabilities. Save and invest. Don't buy an expensive car or watch to simulate success but instead spend money on doing the things that actually *make* you successful: learning and development. When you decide to invest in becoming the person your dreams require, that momentum builds, and it's contagious. Suddenly, you are not just the person who achieved their goals but a role model for so many others.

Belief #3: Be a Role Model in Your Own Life Before Setting Expectations for Others

If you're reading this book, I assume you want to live among the 1%. You want to be at the peak. You want to have joy, health and wealth. You want to build great relationships, and you want to make great money. If you want to become the best version of yourself, then you must be a role model in your own life.

Many business owners say they want a successful, profitable business that runs like a well-oiled machine but without modeling the Miracle Hour for their team. Business owners will come to me and ask, "Can't I just hire someone to do that?" Yes, but if done too soon, this is a crucial mistake. I have a full team across multiple companies that executes on the Miracle Hour and makes sales without me each day. But I poured into that team first. I walked side by side; I coached, trained, modeled and invested in building the systems and ecosystem to set them up for success. So, yes, you can hire someone to do it for you, but make sure you are not setting them, and your company, up for failure.

Leadership means modeling, living by the systems, processes, plans and inroads for success that you and you alone have established. Offloading the work without systems in place and providing training will only lead to failure.

Being a role model means going first. I have this conversation with my daughter all the time. You don't need to have all the answers, but you do need to have the willingness to try. You have to commit to putting one foot in front of the other and to learning through failure every step of the way. That is how you become the person your dreams require.

Belief #4: Scale Comes from Doing the "Unscalable"
When I started teaching the Miracle Hour, I would tell my clients that this is so simple a middle-school student could do it. Now, of course, Madison is living proof of that. I am watching as an 11-year-old executes the very principles I teach business owners to be successful: velocity, momentum, creating transferable systems. These are the steps to scaling.

People often think that scale comes from massive undertakings: more automation, more technology, less direct involvement in the business. And these things *do* come with growth. But you can only scale when the foundation is already working.

Though it may sound counterintuitive, you have to start by doing the unscalable first. One of the biggest traps that today's entrepreneurs fall into is the temptation to automate, evergreen and systematize something that isn't even working. For instance, an entrepreneur may want to automate their sales process — even if they're not selling anything. An entrepreneur may decide to evergreen a webinar that isn't converting. They want to create a sales funnel when they're not even making sales on the phone with people.

Scale comes from building in a repeatable, transferable way. And the Miracle Hour is infinitely repeatable and transferable.

As I mentioned earlier, I run a live Miracle Hour with my team every single day. By 9 a.m., I'm on Zoom with my team and we're executing the steps of the Miracle Hour together across companies. Every team member across sales, marketing and client services participates in their own version of the Miracle Hour, and they make sales without me every single day. In fact, they have generated millions of dollars in sales without me. I've built entire businesses that don't use my face or name — people don't even know I own the company — because I taught them this system, and my employees are building relationships with people. There is momentum and velocity and continuity.

Inside the Miracle Hour toolkit, I break down how team member across roles and departments can leverage their own variation of the Miracle Hour to support and drive profitability in your business. To download it for free, visit https://www.thekellyroach.com/miracle.

As business owners, we need transferable systems because the most dangerous number in business is one. If you're the only salesperson, that poses an enormous problem because life happens: health emergencies, family situations, etc. You need other people in the business besides you who know how to sell. But without putting in the effort to lay the basic groundwork, creating those transferable systems is impossible. Too often I encounter business owners seeking to outsource sales before implementing any real system for it first.

That's why it's imperative that you focus on mastering the unscalable things first. Enter the Miracle Hour, which is extremely transferable and, thus, extremely powerful. It's a momentum-driving machine. When you have a clear path for getting the desired results and can train your team to execute, sales don't have to rely on you 24-7.

Many people confuse scale with growth. Growth is doing more. Scale is identifying efficiencies where you can do more with *less* resourcing. You don't have to keep spending the same amount of time, money, energy, effort, tools or resources to get bigger and better results. From a sales perspective, with the Miracle Hour, the momentum builds like a snowball. That's how you go from one sale a day to two sales a day, from five sales a day to 10 sales a day. It's not necessarily about more effort but about the momentum and velocity that comes at scale.

Belief #5: When Someone's Not Paying You, You Have Nothing to Lose

I started my corporate career in an entry-level sales and recruiting position and worked my way up the corporate ladder, getting promoted seven times over the course of eight years with the company. From there, I hired, trained, recruited, managed and led sales teams of as many as 100 people. When I started leading, a key piece of advice that I shared with every salesperson I trained was this: When someone's not paying you, you have nothing to lose.

What can you lose if someone's not giving you their money? Nothing. This should be paradigm shifting, yet entrepreneurs still resist making mistakes even when there's not a single dollar on the line. I think I understand why.

In school, we were taught that every failure would condemn us to a lifetime of even greater failures. If you failed a test, you'd fail a class. From there, your GPA would plummet and you wouldn't get into a good college, which would ruin your chances of graduating and landing a well-paying job. For 20 years, we were all programmed to believe that if we failed, our lives would be irrevocably ruined.

Getting to the root of these fears is important. If we don't talk openly about the origins of these beliefs, we won't shift our mindsets. You can't develop a millionaire mindset unless you tap into the reason why you fear failure, why you believe you're at risk if you try something and it doesn't go well. Harboring such fears doesn't make you a weak or incapable person; it doesn't mean that success isn't possible or that there's something wrong with you. For decades, you've been indoctrinated into this belief system, but now it's up to you to choose to release yourself from it. Why? Because in the entrepreneurial world, failure is the stepping stone to success.

Not only is failure a given, but it's also one of the best ways for you to learn. By running hundreds of tests, seeing what works and what doesn't, you extract invaluable information. You learn how to succeed.

Belief #6: The Millionaire Mindset Is a Growth Mindset, Not an "I Made It" Mindset

Once you overcome that fear-of-failure hurdle, build momentum and start seeing traction, you might think you've finally "made it." Wrong. The millionaire mindset is a growth mindset, and one that is crucial to hone at every stage in the game. Over the years, I've noticed something surprising happen to many entrepreneurs once they obtain a certain level of success. All is going well then suddenly their confidence starts to plummet. Why? Maybe they are experiencing more brand visibility than they anticipated and are therefore fielding criticism from others. Maybe their business has become far more complex, they're managing greater expenses or their team is growing. They quickly realize that in order to maintain performance and continue growing, they need to master a new set of skills — skills they may or may not possess.

Success inevitably comes with new challenges and frustrations. You have to constantly evolve and push yourself — and ignore naysayers and haters. There will be problems and challenges at every level. What worked for years may suddenly stop working. You may have to roll up your sleeves and get scrappy again to figure out what works.

No matter what storm you're weathering, it's crucial that you keep elevating yourself. Ask yourself whose opinion matters most. Hopefully the answer is God. Perform for an audience of one. It's between you and your creator to become everything you're capable of being based on the talents and gifts instilled in you. With that North Star, my top priority is showing up as the best version of myself. Second to that is showing up for the people I'm here to help. If you're more worried about what random people on the internet say about you than the people whose lives will be changed by your work, you're never going to succeed. Know who you're showing up for and whose opinion counts. The opinions that count belong to those who want, need and can afford your products and services. Your job is to add value for them, to show up for them and to keep learning and developing the skills to do so.

Entrepreneurs at every stage in their careers need these reminders. Over the years, I've watched entrepreneurs reach incredible financial milestones, grow their teams, make investments, increase ad spend, and then all of a sudden, business halts. They're not making *any* money. They have a brand new set of challenges. Instead of embracing those new challenges, though, their confidence takes a nosedive. They'll think, "Maybe I should retreat." I've seen that happen at $1 million, then again at $2.5 million and then again and again. It happens at every level.

A lot of people's answer to those hurdles is to lower the bar, change the goal or give up on the dream; they pull back. Then, unfortunately, they still experience pain, but now it's due to not reaching their potential.

Clients often share their fears of growing their businesses and of what *could* happen. They fear team issues, client challenges, etc. I always explain that you can never play small enough to secure the peace because most likely all those things will happen anyway. It doesn't get easier; we get stronger. Go for what you really want and don't let fear hold you back.

Pulling It All Together
Throughout this chapter, we've discussed what it takes to be the person your dreams require, mastering the unscalable and making sure that you're investing in and learning from people who have your best interest in mind. We've discussed how to close the gap between what you say you want and what you're actually modeling. We've examined why it's necessary to show up as the person that your dreams require. My client Julie's story perfectly encapsulates these lessons.

When I met Julie, she had recently started her business after leaving a seven-figure corporate career in the Fortune 500 world. Before working with us, she was making just around $45,000 per year with no profit — she was reinvesting everything in order to grow. Very quickly, we were able to help her generate her first six figures as an entrepreneur. In just 18 months, Julie built a $1.4 million coaching business.

Even though she was having great success in my program, Julie got caught up in the online noise — automated funnels and shortcuts — and decided to explore other strategies. In that time, things inevitably began to stall.

This past year, she came back to work with us again, and ever since, her business has exploded. She has already brought in over 700 new customers. She's grown her business by over $1 million and she's continuing to thrive.

She once said to me, "Please don't let me ever fall into those traps again because it is very tempting." And she's right — it *is* tempting. An entrepreneur's work is hard work, and this is why having faith is imperative. The harder path is often the right one. Success achieved over time is success that lasts.

> *"We have TRIPLED our revenue in 12 months!"*
>
> *-Julie Ciardi, founder, IGNITE HER®*

If you believe in yourself, you will see miracles play out in your life, but you have to show up and play to experience them.

Most of the time, the right choice is also the hard choice. It's doing the work. It's staying the course. It's knowing that if you do the right thing for the right reason, you'll reach your goal just like Julie did.

For years now, I've had the privilege and honor of being the catalyst for so many people making their dreams come true. I'm not just talking about business dreams, either. I'm talking about the dreams that we hope to realize because of the wealth we accumulate through our work: traveling around the world with family, retiring spouses, paying off debt, funding college and building vacation homes. One of my clients saw her parents' house destroyed in a fire. Using the money from the sales methods that we taught her, she was able to rebuild her parents' home.

If you want to be a blessing to other people, it starts with one hour a day. For one hour, do the right thing to advance your business. Then, when an opportunity to be the blessing in someone else's life comes, you're well positioned to do so.

If you are ready to get started implementing the Miracle Hour for your business, visit https://www.thekellyroach.com/miracle to download your free Miracle Hour toolkit and get started with the full structure, templates and examples right away.

Chapter 4: Take Back Your Most Important Asset: Your Time

So many entrepreneurs struggle with time management because we spend time on things that don't actually matter. As I mentioned at the beginning of this book, one of the first things I did when I began building my business was get support from interns.

One day a week, for one hour at 7 a.m., I would meet with my intern, Nicole, at the local Starbucks before going into the office. She took everything off my plate that was not directly tied to profits so that I could focus on the only two things that keep a business running and growing: getting customers and serving existing ones. As a founder, it's so important that you identify what you — and only you — can do. Those things that fall in your zone of genius. Everything else should be insourced, outsourced or co-created with someone else.

You cannot do this alone. Start from where you are with what you have. Maybe that's hiring a few people to support you. Personally, I've seen success in starting people out as interns and then eventually bringing them on as full-time employees.

Nicole grew from intern to part-time contractor to my second full-time hire. 10 years later, she has worked in three of my companies, running millions of dollars of business across our portfolio. She's been promoted five times and is one of the most integral team members in my business — building relationships with our customers, generating and closing referral sales, and adding millions of dollars in revenue to the company over the years. Decide the culture you want to create and then empower your team to embody it.

In fact, like Nicole, some of my best employees started as interns, and now they have six-figure-plus roles in my company. It's a win for them, and it's a win for me.

Being brutally honest with ourselves is the key to this entire process. So many entrepreneurs, out of ego, say, "I have to be the one to do it. If I don't do it, it won't get done the right way." Those entrepreneurs don't empower their teams to execute on their behalf. They don't demonstrate trust. As a result, they stay stuck and struggling because they cling to the notion that "it needs to be me" when that's absolutely not the case. Then, when they do hire help, they neglect to train new team members properly. They don't set them up for success; they don't give them the ownership necessary to manage a process end to end.

This is why I wrote *Bigger Than You: The Entrepreneur's Guide to Building an Unstoppable Team*. I saw so many stuck entrepreneurs struggling, spending their time on things that don't actually build a company. With that approach, you'll never build a successful business. In the entrepreneurial space, there's a lack of information and resources on how to build a successful team. Entrepreneurs forget — or never learn — that 85% of their team's success comes down to leadership. Often people believe that hiring someone is the solution without realizing that hiring someone does not mean their business will be successful or that what they're hiring for will add value to the business. It's how an individual is hired, trained, onboarded, managed, led and coached that determines whether they'll be successful and supportive, or not.

You will not build a successful, multimillion-dollar business without help and resources. Whether that means hiring a part-time contractor or interns, *you have to start with where you are with what you have.*

The Costs of Saving Time

Maybe you're reading this, thinking, "I'd love to hire someone or bring on my intern full-time, but where is the money?" If building your team seems like taking an enormous financial leap, take a deep breath. You're not alone.

That said, it's important to keep your rationale in mind. Why are you hiring people in the first place? The answer should be to give you back your time so that you can focus on profit-producing activities and activities that are strictly in *your* zone of genius. The reason companies often struggle to bring on new employees who actually support profitable growth is that the business owner has not done their homework. Before hiring someone, they haven't identified how they're going to tie that role to revenue-generation, let alone how they'll take their own time back and translate it into bigger and better profits.

Enter the Miracle Hour — again. Anyone reading this book can find help for a minimum of one hour a day to get started with a Miracle Hour. Say you hire someone to give you just one hour back each day, and that hire costs $50 an hour. Investing $50 so that you can focus on your Miracle Hour each day — posting content or having conversations with new prospects, existing clients and past clients — will help you generate potentially hundreds of thousands of dollars in revenue. If you're broke and your bank account is empty, barter with someone. Whatever your service or product is, bartering is the most original and basic form of doing business, and it works. Even today as a massive team, we barter. In fact, some of the best partnerships are built on people sharing their experiences and skills to mutually benefit one another.

As the saying goes, dance where your feet are. Too many people make the excuse that they can't stay consistent with the

Miracle Hour because they don't have the time. Millionaires know that we all have the same 24 hours. You never *have* the time, you *find* and *create* the time.

Start by architecting how you'll get from where you are to where you want to be. Begin by identifying what you need to take off your plate so that you can focus on profit-producing activities. Who should own these tasks? Is there someone on your current team, or do you need to make a new hire?

Once you find someone who can help take things off your plate, determine how you can make that person successful. Because if it's a win for them, it's a win for you. I tell my clients this every day: No one wants to suck. No one wants to fail. But many entrepreneurs and small business owners hire people only to be frustrated with the results — frustrated by what those people aren't contributing. If you have an employee who's struggling, there's a very high likelihood that training, development, coaching, mentorship and accountability are lacking. Of course, if you're checking all five of those boxes and the person is still struggling, that person probably doesn't belong in your company. Before jumping to that conclusion, though, ask yourself, have I set up this person for success?

What actions do you need to take right away to ensure your team can take ownership of the things you need taken off your plate?

In *Bigger Than You*, I break down the process for hiring, coaching, training, leading and managing people so they can run entire companies for you. That may sound like the other side of the rainbow, but it is possible. I have done it and you can too!

Overcoming Resistance
In the process of bringing others on board to take back your time, it's common to encounter friction or resistance. Yet, surprisingly,

that resistance doesn't come from other people — it comes from you.

Grab your copy of Bigger Than You: The Entrepreneur's Guide to Building an Unstoppable Team

Yes, it's often faster and easier to do a task ourselves. It's more comfortable, too. In five minutes, you could do what might take an hour to train someone else to do. But, in a sense, that's a lazy attitude. And laziness is what keeps us doing things that we could — and should — empower other people to do.

As an entrepreneur, you must choose between doing what's most expeditious and what actually advances your business and your life.

As I've mentioned, when I was first starting my business, I had next to no time. I credit that lack of time with putting into perspective the scale of my dream. It was a huge dream. More than anything, I wanted to be home with my family. My driving force was exiting the corporate world and retiring my husband, Billy, so we wouldn't have to put Madison in day care. I was traveling all over the country every three weeks, and as a mother, this was untenable. I wanted to be home. I wanted to be present for the moments with my daughter, with my family. For me, that short-term sacrifice of being hyper-vigilant, of being clear on where I needed to focus my time and where I needed to get support, allowed me to cross the bridge to freedom.

Just the other day, I was working in the front room of my house, listening to Billy play music in his studio while Madison was upstairs getting ready for dance class. We had just finished homeschooling for the day and I thought, "My God, we're exactly where we're meant to be." And while that's true, it came from 20 years of deciding to become the person my dreams required me to be. Lay the bricks, build the foundation, and all your dreams will come true.

You can have whatever you want, but you have to get out of your own way.

That's why I emphasize the value of being clear on your dreams. I became good at time management precisely because I was clear on *my* dream. I believe the family unit is the most important structure in society, and my dream was to keep my daughter out of day care. I wanted to be home with my family. I wanted my husband to be home with our family. I wanted our family to live in a peaceful, happy home.

To every entrepreneur reading this book, I encourage you to dig deep and identify what lights that fire inside. What is most sacred to you in life? What inspires you to choose the harder thing over the comfortable thing? What is the life you dream of living?

The average adult makes 35,000 decisions a day. In other words, we have 35,000 chances a day to make our dreams come true. The Miracle Hour is about dedicating at least one hour of decision-making time to that endeavor.

Frequently, I hear entrepreneurs say they don't have time to focus on money-making activities. My response to them is simple: There's nothing else for you to do. Every day, I meet entrepreneurs who tell me they don't have time to do the Miracle Hour. I wonder what exactly these entrepreneurs are doing.

At its core, a business has only two functions: getting clients and serving existing clients. If you're not running an eight- or nine-figure business with thousands of customers, all you have is time. If you are under the impression that you don't have time, that means you're spending your time on activities that don't meaningfully move the business forward.

Remember that exercise in Chapter 1 where you identified all the activities that are directly tied to customer acquisition and service/retention versus everything else? Imagine everything else disappeared. In that scenario, you would have eight hours a day to focus on building and growing your business. (By the way, retaining customers is a business-building activity that can lead to enough referrals to double your business year over year, if you use the Miracle Hour wisely for this purpose). Ultimately, you would have more money, more fun, more joy, more fulfillment and more meaning in your business — and you'd reach your goals faster.

If you're reading this and feeling like you don't have time for the Miracle Hour, I want you to flip through your calendar. Look at what's occupying your time. Ask yourself, *Are these things getting me a new customer or keeping the ones that I have?* If the answer is not an explicit yes, then that activity should be paused.

Now, that doesn't mean you have to cease that specific activity forever. In your life and in your business, there are seasons. There will be seasons where you do more of certain activities, and seasons where you do less of others. But if you're in a season as an entrepreneur where you're not yet earning the income you'd like, your first priority has to be increasing your retention rate with your current customers and acquiring new ones.

Remember: Successful entrepreneurs *create* the time. We all have the same number of hours in the day. What will you choose to focus on in those hours? Because what you choose to focus on is what makes your life.

The Three Tiers of Effective Time Management
Tier One: Outsourcing

Outsourcing is the most fundamental tier of time management. Yet, if you're a seasoned entrepreneur reading this book, you might find yourself tempted to skip over this section. You might be thinking, "I already do that." Let me invite you to stick around.

Because here's the thing, even if you are already outsourcing, that doesn't mean you're optimizing to the best of your ability. Every quarter, I recommend conducting a business assessment. During this assessment, identify every item on your calendar and every task on your desk, and ask yourself, *Where do I need to do a better job outsourcing?*

Outsourcing should happen with anything that someone can do better, faster, cheaper than you can — without posing undue risk to the business. What I must stress is that successful entrepreneurs never outgrow this. This system of time management is predicated on a quarterly practice of dialing back to zero. Every three months, rebuild from the ground and up. If you assess what you're doing and continuously level up your leadership, you'll enhance the power and impact of what you're spending time on.

3 Tiers of Time Management

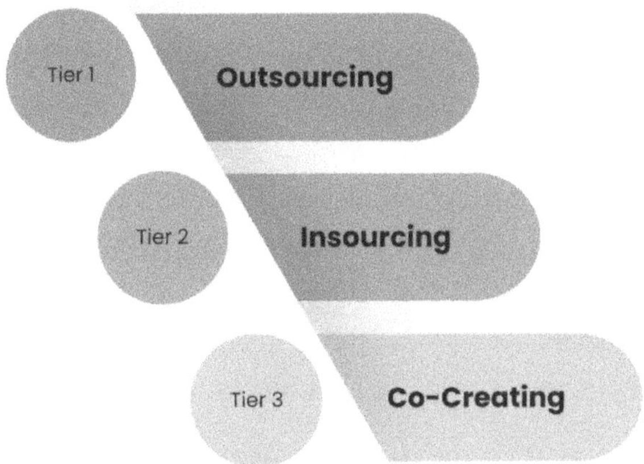

Even those of us who have internal teams need to do this. Sometimes we need to better leverage and empower the team we already have, and sometimes there are tasks that don't make sense to pull your internal team in for and should therefore be outsourced instead. You have to protect your best people's time, just like you need to protect your own.

There's a key difference between giving someone individual tasks as part of a greater process versus owning the end-to-end task from execution to results. When you only recruit people to take on singular tasks, you end up carrying the mental load in your business. Invariably, you'll feel frustrated because you have a team, but you still feel like you're doing it all. Delegating tasks is not synonymous with training for ownership.

Here's the rub: Many small business owners outsource *everything*, but you cannot legally manage outside contractors the way you would employees. So while outsourcing helps to a point, you may eventually need an internal team to take true ownership of driving productivity and profit.

In order to build a truly high-performance team, you will most likely need a hybrid of full-time staff who can own departments, divisions, major projects and programming and outsourced support for overflow tasks. Outsourcing helps to move with speed, stay consistent with profit-producing activities and keep your internal team focused on their highest impact areas.

Action item: Identify what it is you need to outsource now in order to accelerate the timeline of your dream.

Tier 2: Insourcing

After the outsourcing process, there comes a time when you will have more needs. You want things to move faster. You want more ownership, better results. You will get to a point where instead of relying solely on outsourcing, you need a full-time team member dedicated to a specific initiative.

You need to assess when you have taken something as far as it can go in its current form and now needs to be managed in a more comprehensive, hands-on way. This can take something that is already working and exponentially accelerate it. This could be applied across departments: sales, social media management, content creation, finance operations, etc.

For example, we brought advertising in-house for our company many years ago. A lot of entrepreneurs still outsource advertising. Then they get frustrated because their ads perform great until suddenly costs skyrocket and the agency no longer gives that account the time and attention needed to get it back on track. There is a big difference between being one of many clients and someone's full-time, exclusive focus.

Tier 3: Co-Creating

Co-creation is the process of collaborating to get a faster result that's bigger and better. For example, I co-create with a media company, Motivation and Success Network. We work together on various media projects for expanded visibility and reach. I co-create with a stylist; I provide the direction and examples, and she shops and lines up outfits. I even consider my health and fitness journey a co-creation process since I am able to achieve significantly more in a 30-minute session with a trainer than I could on my own. I'm saving time, energy and brainpower.

Sometimes co-creating is hiring a helper for a specific project, like securing a book publishing deal. Sometimes it's investing in a full-time leadership role to serve as your strategic partner. Other times, it's identifying the right collaboration partners so that you win in a bigger way by joining forces.

Action item: Decide what needs to be outsourced, insourced or co-created. Fill in the chart with all the activities that can help you take back your time and grow by leveraging the power of people.

RECLAIM YOUR TIME:

FILL IN THE SHEET BELOW WITH THE ACTIVITIES YOU NEED TO OURSOURCE, INSOURCE, OR CO-CREATE.

OUTSOURCE	INSOURCE	CO-CREATE
ex: tech setup	ex: content creation	ex: publishing a book

What 3 actions can you take right now to better leverage your time and move more quickly towards your goals?

Before we dive into Chapter 5, make sure to grab your Miracle Hour toolkit at https://www.thekellyroach.com/miracle. Inside, you will find scripts and templates for starting conversations and converting various types of business, from upsells to add-ons and from low-ticket offers to high-ticket offers.

Inside The Virtual Business School program, we teach entrepreneurs not only how to systematize daily sales with the Miracle Hour, but how to create no-brainer offers that convert on demand, without requiring sales calls. We call this a "trust-building offer," which is structured differently than your typical low-ticket offer. If you are curious about using a trust-building offer to make daily sales inevitable in your business, visit https://www.virtualbusinessschool.com.

Chapter 5: The Five Types of Sales Every Healthy Business Should Strive For

Earlier in the book, I shared the two core functions of a business: getting new customers and retaining your current customers. There are two core metrics that go hand-in-hand with the Miracle Hour, and they're the most important metrics in determining a business's ability to grow and sustain: customer acquisition costs (CAC) and lifetime value (LTV).

Let me explain: When your CAC is too high, a business can't be profitable even if you are adding new customers on a consistent basis. When LTV is low, that suggests constant churn, which means that even if you're adding customers, you can't keep up with the turnover. As a result, you're constantly chasing new customers and struggling to grow your revenue.

Most entrepreneurs focus mainly on acquiring new customers. They direct most of their energy toward sales and marketing, which is important but costly if the back end of your business (aka existing clients) is neglected. While new customers are crucial, the reality is, they are seven times more expensive and take seven times more manpower, time, energy, effort and money than selling to an *existing* customer. Selling to an existing customer means renewals, upsells, add-ons, etc.

Business owners experience burnout and cash flow issues as a byproduct of chasing the wrong things instead of installing systems around the right ones. Remember, the Miracle Hour is a set of five to seven impact activities that you'll do in a specific quantity every day to consistently make sales in your business. It's designed to remind business owners that when you look at making sales in your business every day, there are a multitude of simple ways to make it happen. In fact, four of the five categories of sales that you want to make every single week in your business using the Miracle Hour should not rely on new customers (unless you are in a marketing-related role). This is where The Miracle Hour toolkit comes in handy in helping you decipher how each department and role can contribute to the Miracle Hour in their own way. Download it here: https://www.thekellyroach.com/miracle.

The five types of sales you should focus on weekly are:

1) ***Reactivations***, or bringing back past customers to work with you again;

2) ***Upsells***, or adding on a new service for an existing customer that will increase their lifetime spend with you;

3) ***Referrals***, or having a pre-existing customer introduce you to another customer, in essence coordinating the sales process for you;

4) ***Renewals***, or seeing current customers resubscribe or renew their contract; and

5) ***New Customers***, or customers who have never worked with you before.

Do the math. Based on these proportions, 80% of the sales you should aim to make weekly come from engaging *current* customers in one way, shape or form.

The Miracle Hour, an activity that you're doing daily, suddenly becomes a lot easier than you thought because you're not spending all your time, money, energy and effort chasing new customers. Your Miracle Hour activity should be spread across current customers and past customers — those who will champion your work and drive new customers through referrals. Then you can focus on new customers.

Operating under the belief that you have to find a new customer every day in order to make a sale every day can be overwhelming. But when you realize that much of what you're doing in the Miracle Hour is retaining relationships, staying in active conversations with current and past customers, developing ways for current customers to help create *new* relationships through referrals, and sustaining the conversation with people who've expressed interest but haven't bought in yet, this equation becomes wildly simple. Achieving one sale a day can involve nothing more than building on pre-existing relationships, then leveraging them to build new ones.

This is why I emphasize, and re-emphasize, your two core activities: getting customers and serving the ones you have. So many business owners get derailed by chasing larger revenue numbers when they could double or triple their income by increasing their retention rate. Imagine two business owners who both have the potential to do $1 million in revenue. One business owner takes home $500,000 a year. The other business owner is only taking home $100,000 a year. The difference between these two entrepreneurs comes down to how fully they embrace serving their current customers. Are they retaining those customers? Upselling them into higher-tier programs as they advance? Renewing them for another year? Making it easy for them to make referrals by providing affiliate codes or swipe copy and graphics to share about upcoming workshops, product releases or sales?

Yes, both business owners need to bring in new customers — that will always be part of the equation. But too many businesses lose money out the back end no matter how they spend on the front end because recurring revenue is stagnating.

The Miracle Hour is an opportunity to refocus. You cannot get retention, renewals, upsells, reactivations and referrals if you're not doing a good job servicing your customers and staying in touch with them. Since four of the five categories of sales hinge upon you building great relationships with your customers, retaining those relationships and continuing to deliver results, you can tune out the outside noise that tells you to prospect indiscriminately. In this way, the Miracle Hour keeps you accountable for doing exceptional work.

As entrepreneurs, especially those who serve a premium clientele, we have to remember that people are busy. They have their own priorities, which means they need to be constantly reminded of the value you represent. It's your job to constantly bring them back to their "why."

We lose 80% of what we retain immediately. I see this all the time. Customers come to us and get an incredible result or ROI. As they start raising their standards, they tend to forget where they were when they came to us in the first place. If you, as the business owner, aren't going back and reflecting their progress and success they've achieved as a result of your programs or services, those customers lose sight of how much you've impacted their journey and their results. That's a problem. Who will want to spend *more* money with you if they no longer recognize the value you've already added for them? That's why tracking customers' progress, whether by measuring customer results or conducting customer satisfaction surveys, is key.

Activity vs. Activation
I've never met a business owner who wasn't "busy." Business often comes from the activities that take up most of our time day to day. Activity, on its own, does not always equate to sales. Activation, on the other hand, is *deliberate* activity. It involves making a specific invitation with a specific outcome in mind, one that advances both the business and the person in front of you.

The truth is, activity can now easily be accelerated, or automated entirely using AI.

The future of AI is unfolding right before our eyes, and we are witnessing firsthand how emerging tools and technology is replacing operational tasks entirely, which means that your time is no longer best spent on "busy work" – it's best spent on conscious, intentional relationship-building and creation.

While slowing down to be intentional doesn't always feel like the most productive thing we could be doing, the activities that once made us feel productive are no longer a measure of our hard work or productivity.

The difference is monumental.

Activity is frantic:

"I'm going to post a bunch on social media because I've been neglecting it for a week."

"I need to respond to this person because my inbox is piling up."

Activation is *intentional*:

"I'm going to post about my lead magnet with the goal of driving list growth."

"I'm going to use my Miracle Hour to follow up with the top 20 prospects I'm in conversation with who are closest to buying."

"I'm going to send out an email with a specific call to action to book a free consultation with my team."

"I'm going to post a story with a call to action for people to direct message me to get exclusive access to my new offer."

Activation hinges on invitation. Most business owners throw spaghetti at the wall. Don't get me wrong, they're doing a ton of *activity*. They're taking a ton of *action*. They're working extraordinarily hard. But there's no activation because there's no intention. The Miracle Hour is designed to help you transform that activity into tangible, predictable results. The Miracle Hour gives you a process to follow every day to make sure you don't get stuck in the activity trap (where 99% of business owners are caught) versus activation, which is inspiring someone to take action that leads to a specific outcome and result.

It's truly you against you every single day. We often get distracted by the things that make us *feel* productive when the most important things are not the five-alarm fires that we think we need to put out in that very moment. There's a big difference between *feeling* productive and *being* productive. It's a lot easier for an entrepreneur to say, "I'm going to mark these 20 mindless tasks off of my list," than to say, "I'm going to intentionally reach out to 100 people that I want to make an offer to." The former is easier. The latter requires faith and unwavering conviction. You have to trust that you'll do the right thing for the right reason, and you'll ultimately see the returns.

How do you make the Miracle Hour predictable? How do you guarantee consistent results? You build based on metrics. This is an age-old basis of business growth.

In one of our recent homeschooling sessions, I was teaching Madison about metrics. Here's how I explained it to her: Metrics are input. What you put *into* the business dictates what you get *out* of the business.

I'll use the Courage Club as an example. Madison wants to enroll 400 members by the end of this year. Right now, she has 50 members, which means she has to grow by seven members per week in order to reach her goal by the end of the year. Therefore, the output she wants is seven members a week.

Your metrics are simply a set of defined activities that you'll do to achieve your desired outcome. The optimal number of activities is five to seven. These activities are closest to the money; they're the activities most likely to get you to your goal.

Whenever we post a video that Madison has recorded for social media, the call to action is, "Comment COURAGE for more information." That's how we want people interested in learning about the club to take action. Nearly every video we post drives a sale. Right now, we're posting a video every other week. Soon, Madison will go from one video every other week to one video a day. And guess what will happen then? She'll see one sale a day. But we won't stop there. Madison has six total impact areas to focus on as well because simply getting a lead to express interest is not enough. The follow-up, nurture and referral ask are how you add rocket fuel. Madison's impact areas look like this:

1) Record a video to post on social media;
2) Create a social media story about the club 1 or 2x per week;
3) Go live to the community 1x per week;
4) Send direct messages to people on the interest list to make direct offers to join;
5) Connect with current members in the club; and
6) Send emails.

Each impact area has a quantity, and since Madison only has three to five hours a week to dedicate to the Courage Club, we built her metrics to match this.

It's that straightforward, but people like to make metrics bigger and more intimidating than they really are. If the word *metric* provokes overwhelm or intimidation in you, change the language: input, activity or profit producer. No matter what you call it, these are the defined actions you'll take every single day, every single week, to reach your goal.

Determining how many of those activities you need to do in order to yield the output you want from your business may require trial and error. I encourage you to start wide and test multiple things to determine which are the biggest drivers for results. From there, focus on doing more of what you know works.

Take a moment to review your last 50 customers. Where did they come from? A live masterclass? A launch? Your email list? A referral? Are they reactivations of past customers?

When you look at your history and observe that 80% of your last 50 customers came from one source, clearly that source should become your top priority. By multiplying the activity, you'll multiply the outcome so long as you retain integrity and quality in that activity. Start with the lowest hanging fruit in the area that has produced the biggest results and go down the list from there.

What are the top three client-generators that you want to multiply and scale intentionally with the Miracle Hour based on previous, proven success?

1: ____

2: ____

3: ____

Strategizing Success: How to Guarantee the Five Types of Sales Actually Happen

I can't emphasize enough the importance of starting with the end in mind. When you reverse engineer from your desired outcome — whether that's a dollar amount or a shift in the scope or focus of your work — so much falls into place. Remember, the five types of sales you're aiming for are prospects (or new customers), reactivations, referrals, renewals and upsells.

To be sure you cover your bases, begin the Miracle Hour by gathering a list of your current customers and a list of your past customers. These lists are invaluable to your business. If you assemble these lists and decide that, during your Miracle Hour on a biweekly cadence, every current and past customer will get a touch point from you, you'll be ahead of 99.9% of businesses.

What should that touchpoint actually consist of? It doesn't need to be complicated. You might check in with current customers to see if you can help them solve a current problem or challenge they're facing, or if they know of anyone who'd benefit from your service. If you consistently reach out to your past and current customers, your business will grow, no slick sales process required. No mindset manipulation or special script. By being a human of integrity, who maintains relationships with people who have paid you in the past and people who are paying you now, your business will multiply.

Imagine a doctor who takes the time to call after a surgery and see how a patient is recovering. Likely, you would hold that doctor in high regard and recommend them to your friends and family. The same holds true in business, regardless of industry.

I hope that, as you're reading, you're breathing a huge sigh of relief. After all, it's so much faster, easier and less expensive to realize daily sales when you're targeting your current and past customers, or when you're getting upsells, renewals, referrals and reactivations. If you don't need to rely on that sliver of new customers, growing your revenue becomes manageable.

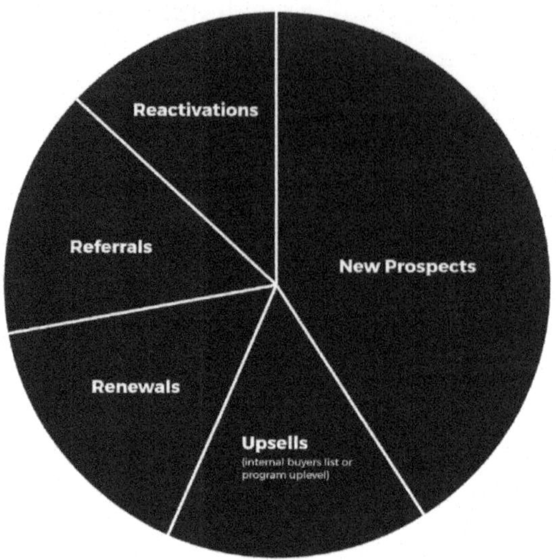

Figure 5.1

Action Items From This Chapter

Step One: Put your current customer list into a spreadsheet, or tag them in your CRM.

Step Two: Create a list of your past customers and add them to the spreadsheet.

Step Three: Review the following pie chart of the five types of sales that you should be striving for on a weekly basis.

Step Four: Ask yourself what offer you'd make for each category.

Think about incentives you could offer clients who are renewing for the second or third year. Maybe it's a bonus call with you or a discounted maintenance price. For clients who are no longer active, maybe you can offer them a jumpstart in the program with specific content to get them ahead quickly.

Offers I could make to current, active customers:

____

____

____

Offers I could make to inactive customers (alumni or past clients):

____

____

____

Offers I could make to referrals:

____

____

____

Offers I could make to clients who are up for renewal:

____

____

____

Offers I could make to prospects:

____

____

____

Make it a goal to generate a sale every day in one of these five categories. Identify your offers, take action accordingly and build that action into your daily Miracle Hour cadence.

I often meet entrepreneurs who fear AI and other technological advancements. Whether it's updates to social media or shifts in search engine algorithms, they worry about keeping up with seemingly endless changes. What's beautiful about the Miracle Hour is that it's an evergreen and agnostic strategy based on concepts that hinge on human relationships. The core activities can be done in hundreds of different formats, regardless of where, when or how you're running your business. It doesn't matter what AI, algorithm changes or new technology is introduced — these are timeless principles that will help you succeed because you are building relationships with humans in a meaningful way. There's no right or wrong strategy, only whether or not you are taking action.

Have you grabbed the Miracle Hour toolkit yet? If not, head to https://www.thekellyroach.com/miracle to get started right away with done-for-you scripts and templates to make sales during your Miracle Hour, regardless of what platform you're using. Inside, you'll find word tracks for content (from stories to emails to feed posts), nurture conversations (texts and DMs) and direct offers.

Chapter 6: The Seven Core Miracle Hour Activities That Make Daily Sales Possible

The Miracle Hour can be adapted to any business or industry, whether you run an online or brick-and-mortar business or its service- or product-based. While we can't ignore the fact that whether you run a business online or offline, your customers are spending time online– we are already actively seeing more and more buying trends move offline.

In today's business environment social media is obviously a crucial part of success, and purchases are influenced by social media to some degree. The average adult spends more than two hours a day on social media. Before someone hires a consultant, books a reservation at a new restaurant or buys a product, odds are, they are using social media to vet that purchase first.

Social media is a superhighway for sales, however, you must be aware of how the integration of AI will affect where people with money merge their time, and how they make buying decisions moving forward.

You can no longer rely on your marketing to do the selling for you. Marketing must do exactly that – market.

Human interface, however, is how you create results.

I know this probably isn't the message you want to hear, but it's critical to focus on building for today while also creating a bridge that sets you up for tomorrow – and that's why relationships are the currency of now.

The good news is this:

Your Miracle Hour is not restricted to any one platform, tech tool or strategy. It is completely adaptable across the board, whether you are using LinkedIn, Instagram, Facebook, X, Substack, or purely analog strategies. I want you to use The

Miracle Hour to make money every single day, and that's imminently achievable so long as you first clarify your 7 core Miracle Hour activities – and then commit to them as a daily non-negotiable.

The 7 core activities will look different from business to business, and are fully dependent on your model and goals.

For online businesses, this might look like:

Step one: Posting on social media to signal to buyers that you're "open for business" (i.e active on social media)

If you run a coffee shop, how do you let customers know you're ready to sell those americanos? You flip on the open sign. Online businesses — and brick-and-mortar businesses who want to attract clientele online — need to do the same thing. The way you turn on the open sign in the online world is to signal to your market that you're open for business.

There's nothing worse than searching for a service provider or a business owner and going to their social media page only to discover there's no current activity. Immediately you think less of that business. You might think that business owner isn't active online. Maybe they'll be slow to respond if you have a question. Maybe they're not focused on growing right now. It's that last assumption that's the most damaging and, perhaps, telling. If you're not committed to your own growth, will you be committed to your customers' growth? Probably not.

Whether you publish a post or share video content, think of your action as a declaration that you're open for business and actively pursuing growth. Feel free to experiment and mix things up. You might rotate between a nurture post, an invitation post or an engagement post. (You can learn more about what I call "hope," "how-to," and "conviction" based posts in my book, Conviction Marketing.)

Step two: Creating top of mind awareness for the top 20 prospects you want to close by engaging on their content, sending a direct message, or swiping up on their story.

As you know by now, I'm a big proponent of the fundamentals. So let's go back to Sales 101. Identify the top 20 prospects that you'd love to work with — people who want, need and can afford your service — and engage with them online. I already discussed the two most important lists in your business, which are your active and inactive customer lists. The third most important list is of those who expressed interest in your services and were qualified but didn't buy. This list is pure gold. If you go back to the sales stats we shared in earlier chapters, then you understand that a significant portion of your sales are sitting on this list, simply waiting for you to follow up.

Many people believe that staying in touch with their top prospects (which is how I prefer to frame "following up") means being pushy. They believe that staying in touch is inherently aggressive or annoying. Instead, I encourage you to challenge your beliefs and reframe this. Staying in touch is really a way of creating top-of-mind awareness.

Top-of-mind awareness is a proven business principle that indicates that people tend to buy from one of the last three providers they were in touch with. In other words, you're keeping your presence known. It doesn't mean you're making an offer every time you get in touch with your top prospects. You might reconnect and ask a personal question if you have had prior conversations. "How was your vacation? How is abc/xyz project progressing in your company?" These are simple, human interactions. If you have a list of prospects that you would love to work with, the most important thing that you can do is stay top of mind for them, or even better, actively invest in building a relationship. People buy on their own terms. When they're ready, you'll be the person who comes to mind for them.

In the online world today, one of the easiest ways to stay top of mind for someone is to engage with their content. Every time you engage with someone's content, you give them a gift. Because when you engage with someone's content, it triggers the algorithm to show it to more people. The fastest, easiest way to get anyone to pay attention to you is by engaging with their content in a meaningful way. No spamming, no pitching. Simply leave a thoughtful comment that adds value or supports them in some way. Repost them and share why their post resonated with you. Again, no need to pitch your services every time you interact with a prospect. These are small but intentional ways to make deposits in the reciprocity bank.

> *"Step two of the Miracle Hour landed me a meeting with a possible referral partner for my bookkeeping business!"*
>
> *-Anonymous Virtual Business School Member*

Step three: Going back through old posts and one-word marketing threads to re-engage commenters who once expressed interest in whatever that particular post was promoting.

Over the last decade, one of the biggest breakthroughs I've witnessed in online marketing is the ascendance of what I call "one-word marketing." This deceptively simple strategy has the power to almost instantly attract and engage your audience. Here's how it works: Create a post and invite people to comment a specific word if they're interested in that topic. Take the example I shared earlier of Madison's Courage Club. Every other week, I publish a post that says, "If you're the parent of a daughter age seven to 14 and you want to help your daughter become a great leader, have the courage and confidence to pursue big goals and do incredible things in the world, comment Courage to learn about the club." (By the way, if you are a parent of a young girl, head on over to https://www.thecourageousbrand.com and get your daughter registered!)

This simple strategy has elicited nearly all our members, but there's a catch. Dropping a one-word marketing thread and passively waiting to see what happens yields sporadic, unpredictable results. Follow-up is a must. That includes replying to their comment directly on the post (you can say something like, "Awesome! I just sent you a direct message. Check your inbox!") as well as sending them a message with the requested information or inviting them to take the next step. You can respond directly with links on the post, but this will depend on the specific platform you are using (some platforms pose restrictions on clickable links).

The one-word marketing strategy rose, in part, from tools like ManyChat, which enables you to automate responses on Instagram. And while a tool like ManyChat may be great for getting initial automated responses, many people who initially respond never take complete action on the item to which they were responding. We actually use this strategy across all platforms, so most of what we do is fairly manual, but it's worth it because this is where a large portion of our sales and list growth comes from.

Leveraging automation and AI can accelerate results, but be careful not to develop an over-reliance on these tools. Automation can help speed up the initial follow-up, but you still need a process for continuing that follow-up for everyone who doesn't make it over to your list (remember, people are busy, they forget, they often get distracted, and many premium buyers simply will not engage with what they can identify is an automated follow up). Not everyone who comments on your posts will follow through to completion. Even if they do make it onto your email list, that doesn't mean they're automatically going to buy. It's on you to stay on top of them during your Miracle Hour activities.

This is why it's critical that you rework your one-word marketing threads on social media by following up. Now you have segmented lists of people who've already expressed interest (aka warm leads). Keep a spreadsheet with a running list of links to your one-word marketing threads. As you launch new campaigns and initiatives, revisit relevant threads and pull those people back into conversations. For example, if you make a post inviting people to join your free workshop in June, and you host another workshop on a similar topic in August, go back to that post and re-invite everyone who previously expressed interest. These are people who may not have attended, who attended but didn't buy or who forgot to register altogether. It is far easier to hit your goals by leveraging the people who already raised their hand than to constantly look for new people.

Invite those people to take the next step, whether that means bumping their comments on that same thread or reaching out through DM. By following up this way, you'll make countless sales because you're following up with people who've already expressed interest.

Step four: Reactivating past DM conversations that ended because either you or the other person stopped responding

Typically, when a conversation starts, there's an energetic back and forth. Eventually, though, either you or the person you're talking to gets busy and stops responding. What happens next? If you're like most people, you let it fizzle out. And guess what happens? Nothing. Absolutely nothing. You could think of your inbox as a graveyard for unrealized sales, or you could think of it as a series of untapped opportunities. Businesses can grow by millions of dollars by simply devoting one portion of the Miracle Hour to revisiting conversations that fell off and practicing good reengagement techniques.

If you need support getting started, The Miracle Hour toolkit includes outreach templates for direct messages that you can use to reactivate conversations. We want you to be able to get started on your Miracle Hour right away, so head over to https://www.thekellyroach.com/miracle to grab your free toolkit and start using those templates and word tracks.

If the idea of reviving a dead conversation prompts feelings of uncertainty, you're not alone. Many people fear that reengagement will make them look desperate or unable to read signals. But here's the reality: When someone stops responding to you, it means nothing. It's not personal. It's not a reflection of how you communicated with them. It means that person is busy. I remind my clients and team that the better the lead, the busier they are and the more likely they are to stop responding because they have so many other things going on. That person isn't thinking about you because it's not their job to think about you. The only way they'll think about you is if you continue to put your name and your face in front of them.

It's easy to get started. Scroll back a few weeks or months and pick back up on those conversations that went quiet. It's incredible that something as simple as going through your inbox can yield such miraculous results.

Often, people are daunted by sales. As a result, they freeze, paralyzed by overthinking. They wonder: Where do I start? What do I do? But it's important to remember that sales are just the transfer of inspiration. Sales are you being excited to help people and share that enthusiasm, even if time has elapsed.

Once you've spent time reactivating past conversations, set aside time to welcome new followers and connections into your world. Thank them for following you, ask how they discovered you, offer them a resource that will add value in some way. This could be a podcast episode, a guide you put together, or a free training that they can apply right away.

Again, you don't have to think of these word tracks or welcome messages on your own. We've compiled a list of scripts for new conversations, reactivations and nurture inside the Miracle Hour toolkit. Go to https://www.thekellyroach.com/miracle to get access.

> *"This is old school relationship building, and I absolutely love it. You learn how to simplify the sales process. It really works."*
>
> *-Anonymous Virtual Business School Member*

Step five: One mass marketing activity: sending an email to your list, a text to your list of phone numbers, or going live on social media.

Part of your daily Miracle Hour should be reaching prospects, clients or past clients at scale. Every day, pick one mass-marketing action: an email to your list (or a segment of your list), a livestream or maybe a mass text promoting an upcoming training or new freebie or a visibility opportunity (guest podcasting, guest coaching or joint live streaming). This is how you reach people in volume.

Some of our best clients have been passive consumers in our ecosystem. They never answered a direct message until they were ready to buy. Sometimes that looks like months of follow-up with no response. But that doesn't mean they aren't paying attention. Often, these are the same people who are quietly reading your emails, catching your livestreams that pop up on their feed and paying attention — just not actively engaging. I always remind clients that usually the people who engage the most often aren't qualified because they've got a lot of time on their hands to spend online. Your best prospects are busy, and your mass marketing efforts are a great way to reach them even if they aren't directly responsive to your follow-ups.

You can rotate these actions to various segments and tags on your list so you don't hit people with mass marketing in the same way every single day. For example, you might send a text on Monday, an email on Tuesday, go live on Wednesday, collaborate on an Instagram or Substack Live on Thursday and guest coach in a client's community on Friday. Just like that, you've incorporated one mass marketing action every single day without exhausting your email or text list.

Step six: Connecting with new ideal clients through your social media explore page, accounts with overlapping audiences, using lead search tools like Sales Navigator, or following "suggested" profiles.

This portion of your Miracle Hour is dedicated to making sure that your top of funnel is always full. As your brand grows, you start investing in paid advertising, your engagement and reach increases, and your content generates more inbound leads (meaning they discover you and initiate contact). You can then spend less time on outbound lead generation. But, if you're new to the online space or just starting to build your online presence, I recommend dedicating time each day to reaching new people.

Again, while your top priorities are going to be your current customers, past customers and warm leads, you should still constantly work to fill your top of funnel so that you never run out of people to pull down to the close.

How and where do you find these people? Start by identifying who your ideal clients follow or engaging with online. These might be individuals who do similar or complementary work to you. For example, I teach business growth strategy. I don't teach people how to land book publishing deals, but many entrepreneurs and thought leaders are also interested in writing and publishing books. This is what I call an overlapping audience. I might look to connect with service providers who are following and engaging with publishing coaches because they would also be interested in growing their brand and business.

Leverage Instagram's "explore" page or Substack's "for you" feed and follow suggested accounts, or use LinkedIn's feed to see who your current connections are engaging with. There are plenty of ways to discover and connect with new people online — and it's all right at your fingertips.

These are deposits in the reciprocity bank. This portion of your Miracle Hour is not about cold pitching — in fact, that's one of the best ways to turn people off from responding. Simply engage with their posts in a meaningful way, follow or request to connect with them or, optionally, reach out and let them know why you connected.

This is where people make the mistake of being generic. Don't send the same copy-paste message to every new person. Tell them why their recent post landed. What initially drew you to their page? Ask a meaningful question to start a conversation. Think about the messages that land in your own inbox that make you cringe. Don't be that person.

Step seven: Making direct offers through a simple DM follow-up, email or text

Never underestimate the power of the ask. Whether it's an invitation to buy a new offer or to hop on a call and discuss, I often tell clients that real transformation requires investment. When you have skin in the game, you are far more likely to take action to get the desired result. Think about it: How many freebies have you opted in for, only to never actually look at them?

Reaching out and inviting someone to have a quick phone call remains one of the most impactful ways to grow your business, especially in a time when human connection is increasingly rare and many businesses rely on AI chatbots to facilitate conversations. The invitation doesn't have to be fancy. It can be as simple as sending a DM, saying, "Hey, when we last talked you mentioned you were interested in helping your team get more organized with their sales activities to improve their execution. Is this still a priority for you? If so, does it make sense to hop on the phone for a few to connect?"

Miracle Hour for Offline Businesses

For offline businesses, on the other hand, your Miracle Hour might look something like:

Step one: Sending a text or email to your list to signal you're open for business.

This could look like sending an email or text message announcing a limited time promotion, new specials, or simply a reminder of your offerings.

Let people know that you're accepting new clients, what they can expect working with you, and how to take the first step to get started.

Do you take walk-ins? Are your services by appointment only? Should customers call ahead of time, or fill out a form online to get started?

Confused minds always say "no." Signaling to people that you're not only open for business but here's the best way to take action, is how you eliminate confusion.

Step two: Creating top of mind awareness for the top 20 prospects you want to close by sending out a personal text, voice note, or email to connect personally and check in.

Again, this does not have to be a direct offer. This could be as simple as checking in with a client you want to renew and following up on a personal story they shared with you the last time they were in your office.

It might be sending a holiday card in the mail.

While online strategies still might be applicable (i.e friend requesting and engaging with your top prospects on social), you can stay top of mind with a physical mailer or a personal text or email.

> *"The Miracle Hour gave me a simple structure to grow my business. To put my butt in the chair, and focus on the specific growth conversations that generate new business for me. It works!!!"*
>
> *Chris Trammell, Personal Brand Architect for Authors and Difference-Makers*

Step three: Replying to customers and inquiries – answer questions, make relevant add-on offers, and ask for Google reviews

Spend time answering questions about services, booking processes, pricing, etc. as they come in – whether it's through social DMs, website inquiries or voicemails.

If customers had follow-up questions post-services, make sure to reply back and keep the relationship going – so you can recommend add-on services, loyalty rewards, referral incentives and reactivations as it makes sense.

If clients are satisfied, reach out and ask for a Google review so that more potential customers can see the results and impact you are having with current clients.

This ensures no communication is left unanswered, and clients continue to feel your support even after investing money to work with you.

Step four: Follow up with past clients who haven't booked in a while, offering them an incentive to come back in

One simple, "we miss you!" text, email, or physical mailer goes a long way.

We've all left appointments and services satisfied, but the need to rebook immediately doesn't always return right away. Consider offering incentives for your best clients to come back in and do business with you again.

This might be a discounted price on select services, a complimentary consultation for a new service you're offering, or first-access to a new service you plan on rolling out publicly soon.

You might even consider hosting a pop up inner-circle event for your top loyal customers, and invite them back in to connect in person, explore new offerings, and maybe even enter to win a drawing for a free service simply for showing up.

If your model doesn't warrant repeat services within a short period of time, consider simply asking for the review or referral to stay top of mind.

Reach out either online or physically – with a gift or personal letter in the mail – to remind them that you're thinking of them.

Step five: One mass marketing activity

Mass marketing could be an email or text campaign, but it could also look like guest interviewing on a podcast, attending a networking luncheon, sponsoring an event or hosting a booth at a local event, or hosting an open house for current and new customers to stop by.

This is an opportunity for you to meet and connect with potential customers at scale, instead of relying on one-to-one outreach.

Step six: Making direct offers by offering free trials, discounts for loyalty members, extensions, or renewals

Whether it's offers to past customers to come back in, offers to new customers who inquired about services via email or phone call but never followed back up to schedule, or making a special offer to a referral from a repeat client, the business of our day to day often leads us to forget that there are thousands – even millions – of dollars in untapped revenue sitting in follow up opportunity.

Just because someone reached out with a question doesn't mean they'll remember to book.

Just because a client booked consistently for three months straight, doesn't mean they'll automatically book for that fourth.

It's up to you to reach out and make those direct offers.

Step seven: Reach out to collaboration partners

Are there other local businesses with complimentary services that you can partner with? Whether it's hosting a local joint pop up event and offering attendees to explore complimentary services from both businesses, or simply swapping business cards to keep at your front desk, there are endless ways to collaborate with businesses that serve your same customer base.

Consider stopping in in-person to connect face to face, reaching out through social media, or sending a personalized gift and handwritten note in the mail.

Asking The Right Questions To Determine Your "Seven Core Activities"

Now, here's the really cool thing: for many businesses, your seven core miracle hour activities may look like a mix of online and offline activities.

I encourage you to consider ways that you can merge both types of activities into your daily Miracle Hour so that you are both building your brand and attracting customers online, while also investing in highly-curated in-person experiences and face to face interaction. For online businesses that don't have a brick and mortar storefront, you can still leverage pop up events, meetups, lunches, and experiences that bring clients physically into your orbit and allow you to accelerate connections and trust in the process.

Online businesses can leverage strategies like sending physical gifts in the mail, just as much as offline businesses can connect with prospects on social media and mass market through social media livestreams, email and text.

What I want to emphasize is the importance of not putting all of your eggs in one basket when determining how you will run your daily Miracle Hour. Determining what your seven core activities are starts with asking the right questions:

- What is my goal?
- Where do my ideal clients spend time?
- What assets do I have to leverage? (social media, email, networks and communities, in-person events)
- What has historically been your most successful strategy to acquire customers in the past?
- Where have your top most recent ideal customers come from?

- What are the easy and obvious activities that you are not doing currently, but if you started, you'd likely get consistent results right away?

Your seven core activities should include the non-negotiable, highly personalized, and what many would consider "unscaleable" activities spread out across your top, middle, and bottom of the funnel so that you can capture, nurture and ultimately close clients consistently and predictably.

Capturing leads ultimately can be done at scale through advertising and automations, but there is often a human touch required to bring the closing process full circle.

Don't underestimate the power of human connection, nurture, and making personalized offers based on what you know about a particular client. This is what drives scale in the activation era – and you need a balance of all three when identifying your core seven activities that you will execute on a daily basis, whether you are online or offline.

Below are a handful of Miracle Hour activities listed out. Highlight or star the ones you know would move the needle most significantly in your business, and are aligned with your specific goals:

- Scheduling a collaboration article or post and cross-promoting it
- Going live
- Sending personalized DMs, text messages, and emails
- Direct phone calls
- Mailing handwritten notes
- Strategic gifting
- Giveaway collaborations, summits or joint webinars and livestreams

- Engaging on your prospects' content in a meaningful way
- Asking for Google reviews or testimonials
- Reaching out to past customers with a rotating "welcome home" offer
- Mailing books or magazines to top prospects
- Pulling articles or reports and sharing them with relevant contacts
- Resharing and congratulating top prospects on article features, awards and recognitions (supporting a book launch, a magazine feature, or a speaking opportunity)
- Working and re-working "one-word marketing" threads from your social media
- Creating short, 60-second or less customized videos for top leads or inactive customers that you'd love to work with again
- Creating a trends report for your industry or state of the union to add value and sharing personally with top leads
- Referral campaigns that incentivize personal introductions
- Hosting alumni-only events (trainings, meetups, etc.) for past clients
- Collecting user-generated content to repost from current and past clients (testimonials, book reviews, podcast reviews, etc) and incentivizing individuals to share
- Extend invitations to a curated dinner party, pop-up mastermind or meetup that you're hosting (and follow up to past attendees to invite them back)
- Inviting prospects to a masterclass, training, workshop, launch, or virtual event you're hosting
- Share a relevant Youtube video, podcast episode or article with a prospect that is specific to a conversation you've had in the past

Identify which of these activities are the greatest and best match for your business and get going right away!

PERSONALIZED communication is the key. Activities can rotate and repeat. Relationships and trust are built over time.

Your Miracle Hour is about knowing who your dream makers and best buyers are and having a clear, specific and intentional plan to create top of mind awareness, add value to the relationship and keep it moving forward.

Inviting people to a call and then making offers is a staple of sales for an obvious reason: Your sales correlate with the number invitations you or your team make. The vast majority of business owners don't make daily invitations to buy. Instead, they wonder why they're not making daily sales.

Remember, invitation precedes activation. Part of your daily Miracle Hour should involve returning to your leads who are closest to buying. That may mean approaching current customers who are ready to advance to the next step in your ecosystem or reaching out to past customers and updating them about a new offer. It might mean approaching customers who are up for renewal and inviting them to extend their time with you. These people are already in a state of readiness to buy because you're keeping the conversations active, engaging with their content, posting regularly and putting out quality products.

Sometimes my clients reach their bandwidth and need to pass off their customers to another member on their team. This is completely fine and should not be a reason to avoid invitation. If you find yourself needing to transition a lead to another person on your team, reach out and coordinate the initial meeting. Introduce your team member to the customer so your team member can keep the conversation moving forward and support your needs and theirs. Ideally, you're getting permission from the customer to make the introduction as well as facilitating it. If that's not possible, reach out and inform the customer about the transition. Remember, if they're not already paying you, you have nothing to lose.

From coaching thousands of business owners and entrepreneurs, I've learned that our perception of sales, and the congruence between sales and fulfilling our potential, determines how high and how far we'll go. I believe that sales are a sacred process of leading someone to meet their highest potential. Sales help someone else get what they want.

That being said, I've also witnessed how jaded many people are about the very concept of sales. People have had bad experiences, and they've been taught things that are incongruent with the identity, authenticity and integrity they want to lead and build their business with. I wrote *The Sacred Art of Selling* to give people a new framework and a fresh operating system for how to approach sales, one that shows them how they can step into the highest potential for their life and everything that God made them to be. By mastering the sacred art of selling, they can become a steward of other people's potential and center their lives around building an empire that glorifies God, serves people and helps them reach their potential. In the entrepreneurial space, divorce rates are through the roof as well as occurrences of mental health crises and addiction. Why? Because pursuing success at all costs and becoming out of balance in that pursuit costs us everything.

I firmly believe that it doesn't need to be this way. *The Sacred Art of Selling* conceives of an operating system with sales and stewardship at the center, one that will allow entrepreneurs to fulfill their highest potential and help other people do the same. While *The Sacred Art of Selling* has not been released as of writing this book, my entire Substack channel is dedicated to this body of work. Scan the QR code to subscribe and learn more.

Subscribe to The Sacred Art of Selling on Substack

The Sacred Art of Selling teaches entrepreneurs how to lower their stress and build peaceful and profitable businesses by practicing *detachment* in the sales process. People often avoid sales because the process feels stressful and high-pressure. This is where detachment comes in. When you're doing enough of the right things that you don't need to put pressure on anything, you can embrace faith, trust and certainty. The Miracle Hour supports this.

After you've done the Miracle Hour for a period of time, you'll gain enough momentum and velocity that sales will come into your business from multiple directions, in ways that you didn't expect. I hope this relieves some of the pressure that entrepreneurs feel. No one conversation, launch or situation is an *end-all-be-all* when you've garnered enough momentum and velocity from doing the right things so that you can detach. This is absolutely imperative for entrepreneurs hoping to achieve their highest potential. They must be peaceful, centered and grounded in their purpose.

Implementing Your Seven Core Miracle Hour Activities
If you're an entrepreneur who's feeling overwhelmed by the myriad possibilities before you, I offer this advice: Start with one. Pick one action and, to borrow the Nike slogan, *just do it.*

As it turns out, the fitness analogy is apt. Perfectionists and high achievers—two categories into which entrepreneurs frequently fall—often avoid taking action unless they're sure they will perform perfectly. When I work with clients, I often say, "Just pick up the dumbbell." We have to start somewhere. Don't worry about form, just take imperfect action.

Sales are exactly the same. You don't have to complete every step of the Miracle Hour to see results. You can design your Miracle Hour around your specific outcomes. And you don't have to have the whole plan (although I give you the whole plan inside the toolkit). Though you may feel like you're starting from square one, there's no reason to not pick up the dumbbell. In other words, send one direct message. Send one email. Publish one post on social. From there, you stack. Stacking one singular positive action at a time leads to growth. That's how I got my team to the point where they can reach 100 people in an hour, which means ultimately, they are creating 500 quality interactions in one single week. If you interact with 500 people a week in a quality way, you will yield five sales or possibly many more. It's math, input to output.

> *"I followed exactly what you said and tailored it to my business and it is already producing results. Your system works like magic!!"*
>
> *-Anonymous Virtual Business School Member*

Now that we've discussed the seven core Miracle Hour activities, take a few moments to reflect. First, determine where your customers are coming from. Identify where you have the highest level of success. That information will help you prioritize what comprises your Miracle Hour so you can build activities to match (remember the 80/20 rule).

For example, if referrals are a strong income source for your business, and you've been getting referrals without a strategic outbound plan to grow those referrals, you could probably multiply your income quickly just by focusing on referrals during your Miracle Hour.

Top customer sources:

1: ____

2: ____

3: ____

Now, start outlining your five to seven core activities so you'll be positioned for success. What are the top activities that will exponentially increase client acquisition? Revisit the activities from Chapters 1 and 2 when we outlined your Magic Index Card and impact activities. Does anything need to change? List those activities below.

1: ____

2: ____

3: ____

4: ____

5: ____

6: ____

7: ____

Remember to keep it simple. Do more of what works. Focus on multiplying the basics, and you will win.

If you find yourself overcomplicating the activities, the Virtual Business School is a great place to start. With direct access to my team every single month during our live hot-seat coaching calls, you have the opportunity to ask questions and get feedback on designing a custom strategy and action plan that works for your unique business and goals. Head to https://www.virtualbusinessschool.com to learn more.

Chapter 7: Aligning Miracle Hour Activities With Your Growth Objectives

At any given time, there are endless ways to grow your businesses. While this can be energizing, it can also provoke overwhelm and lead many entrepreneurs to get mired in indecision. When there are so many possibilities — people to contact, things to say, activities to do — it's common to fall into stasis and do nothing. In this chapter, I want to inspire you to shift your attitude around having options. Instead of provoking indecision, I believe that identifying strong auxiliary activities in addition to your business's seven core activities will help you maximize your Miracle Hour and truly align it with your growth objectives.

I ended the last chapter by asking you to revisit the 80/20 rule. Where do 80% of your results come from? What 20% of the effort yielded those results? That's the formula around which you build your Miracle Hour. To supplement that equation, it's helpful to have auxiliary activities that you can mix and match into your Miracle Hour database.

Auxiliary activities will not only bring variety to your results, they'll also help you target specific focuses in the business. Let me be clear: These are not *new* activities. They go hand in hand with the core actions we covered in Chapter 6. Instead, think of them as supplemental focuses that support each initiative during your daily Miracle Hour. Let's look closer at these supplemental actions.

Send Out Invitations for Conversion Events
If you're building a business in the online space, chances are you leverage conversion events (think masterclasses, live launches, workshops or webinars) to scale your business. In essence, you're selling one offer to multiple people at once. In this case, you might

dedicate your Miracle Hour to inviting leads to register for such upcoming events. This is critical. Many people rely on running ads to reach cold audiences and forget that only 2-3% of your market is ready to buy at any given time. If you have a forthcoming masterclass or workshop, you want to make sure you're not only relying on cold traffic, but you are actively using your Miracle Hour to invite people back who are likely in that ready-to-buy category. These are people who have been in your ecosystem for a while, have booked consultations with you in the past or have attended workshops but have not yet pulled out their credit cards. This essentially ensures that your live events will convert because you're driving attendance with individuals who are already ready to buy and don't need more time getting to know you and vetting your brand.

> *"Focusing on The Miracle Hour (both me and my assistant) for 4 weeks leading up to our launch made a huge difference for us. I did a soft open cart on Tuesday, and had 8 calls booked before I officially even "pitched" on Wednesday. They all enrolled. It's been the most easeful and fun launch I've ever had!"*
>
> *-Anonymous Virtual Business School Member*

We know that multiple interactions with potential customers are necessary to make a sale. It's the 8th to 12th follow-up, the 20th to 40th impression, that leads to a sale. That means if you're running a masterclass, a launch or a workshop, many people will attend multiple events before they buy. So let your ads bring in the new leads and let your email list bring in existing leads who are interested, but use your Miracle Hour to intentionally reach out to people who you personally want to be there. These should be people you believe are ready to convert and just need that extra push.

Again, this isn't in addition to your Miracle Hour. This could be a form of making a direct offer or connecting with your top 20 prospects. Your auxiliary activities are simply another angle for approaching your Miracle Hour depending on your specific goals and company focus at that time.

Fill Your Events

Another auxiliary Miracle Hour activity is filling your in-person events. For instance, at the time of writing this book, I am driving ticket sales for our Called To Lead event as well as our Legacy Leader Mastermind retreat. For all of our events, we create specific lists of individuals who we want in the room. When you know who you want in the room for your events, all you have to do is invite them. What's wild is how often people running events lose hundreds of thousands of dollars mass marketing those events by running ads, which suck out all the profit, when they could be handpicking their guests and simply inviting them personally. If you use your Miracle Hour to invite the people you want in the room, odds are those people will buy tickets — and you won't tank your profits.

Referral Outreach

Reaching out to people in your network for referrals is another great auxiliary activity. Engaging in referral outreach is as easy as grabbing your phone during your lunch break and sending five text messages to people you recently worked with, saying, "Hey, I hope you're happy with [the offer or product]. We love working with you. Do you know anyone else who is looking to do this kind of work? If so, would you be open to making an introduction?"

Too often, entrepreneurs overthink — and overcomplicate — these interactions. Sending that one-line text seeking a new referral is one of the easiest, most efficacious things you can do. After all, we know referrals spend more, stay longer *and* refer more often. Really, they're your best customers.

Who are five people you can take this action with right now?

1: ____

2: ____

3: ____

4: ____

5: ____

Request Reviews From Happy Clients

The first thing we do in our daily Miracle Hour is request Google reviews. Getting a Google review isn't only permanent, platform-agnostic and searchable, it's also one of the simplest ways to build brand authority. You can leverage Google reviews in your stories and your posts, quote them in your email newsletter or books and share them with prospects who are on the fence about buying.

Google reviews are endlessly excerptible and reusable. Nothing more effectively makes the case for sales than someone else speaking to the power of your product.

In addition to requesting Google reviews from customers, we actively pull up our new Google reviews and review them together as a company during leadership calls. We share them on the screen and read them out loud. Afterward, we reflect on our work, our mission, our vision, our goal. Why are we doing what we're doing? Naturally, we also talk about what people are saying in their reviews and how that impacts how we go to market and sell our products. In essence, what we call out as most meaningful and valuable in our business needs to be integrated into our sales and marketing strategy. From there, we move into our daily Miracle Hour, taking five to 10 minutes to request reviews from people who came to us recently and can share their wins from using our products and programs.

As I mentioned earlier, customers often forget how far they've come. That's because they raise their own standards as their performance excels. For that reason, it's crucial that you document their wins and then invite them to reflect on where they were before and how far they've come with you. This makes it that much easier to upsell them, renew them or invite them to refer people to you. Once again, most of this can be accomplished with a quick text or DM.

A quick aside about the ease factor: Recently, on one of my livestreams, I interviewed a client who's had phenomenal results with the Miracle Hour. My client shared, "I was sitting in bed this morning, shooting off DMs, and people came back to me from my waiting list to say they were ready to get started." I took a moment to marvel at how lucky we are that we can do this from our phones. Too often, we take for granted that we live in such a blessed, convenient, accessible moment. At any time, in any place, you have an opportunity to grow your business. All you have to do is take action.

Create and Post Stories

Bringing people along on the journey with you is one of the best things you can do as an entrepreneur. And, no, this doesn't mean you have to become an influencer and constantly document every aspect of your life. I say that as someone who has absolutely zero interest in becoming an influencer, although I have a very established and substantial brand. You won't see me posting my lunch. I don't share a lot of personal stories about what I'm doing with my family. In fact, when I go out with my family, I leave my phone at home. I don't want my off hours to be spent in constant content creation mode.

But when you're working, you should be creating content. In other words, if you're working, *work*. The day that I recorded this book in studio, I recorded tons of audio to talk about different stories to capture what I was doing — walking into the studio, showing the studio, behind the scenes of recording, who I was with, etc. Based on those stories, people could tell that I take my work seriously and belong to a robust network of thinkers and thought leaders. They learned that I have new material coming, that I'm excited to share with the world.

Like I've said, either social media works for you or you work for social media. If you let it, social media can work for you 24 hours a day. In addition to your daily posts (turning on your "open sign"), think about what you can document behind the scenes to create a sense of connection with your audience. What happened during your client calls today? What did you help people overcome? What are you working on? What client wins are you proud of? Share these throughout the day to reach more feeds.

Get in Front of Other People's Audiences

One of the best ways to grow your brand and get high-intent buyers is to be visible, especially in front of other people's audiences (OPA). I recommend all entrepreneurs include in their weekly action plans for growth, a step dedicated specifically to increasing their visibility by adding value. That could mean appearing on other people's podcasts, teaching or participating in their own communities. This is something I've done for over 10 years, and the trickle-down effect has been enormous. It has bolstered my platforms, generated leads and created customers. Again, this is nothing new. It is simply an extension of your Miracle Hour: mass marketing.

Many people neglect to cultivate their visibility because it doesn't seem to net instant results. It's difficult to measure the impact of going on someone's podcast; that effort doesn't neatly translate to leads or sales. But true marketing isn't always measurable or computable. Cultivating visibility is a long game, and it's an essential piece of attracting high-intent buyers.

If you're working to grow and expand your visibility, part of your Miracle Hour might include reaching out to potential collaborators instead of just leads. Who can you partner with who has an overlapping audience? Can you co-author a Substack article together? Do a podcast swap? Find ways to add value to each other's audience. This is another way of putting deposits in the reciprocity bank. You get to share your brilliance with their audience while giving them the gift of sharing their brilliance with yours. Plus, you just built rapport for the next time you want to ask for a referral.

Assess Current Offerings

Assessing your business's core offerings and where there's room for growth is another fantastic auxiliary activity. For example, in my company, we have prospect lists that are categorized by offer type. My team has a list of prospects they might reach out to and nurture to get them join our Legacy Leaders Mastermind, which is our seven- and eight-figure group. We have prospect lists for our Virtual Business School GOLD program, which is our six- to seven-figure business incubator. Here, we help businesses master selling one-to-many to make bigger leaps, faster, once they have the foundations working. We also have prospect lists for our consulting services, in-person events and retreats, and this makes it much easier to organize our Miracle Hour based on our company objectives.

There are endless activities that you can do to offer someone what you know they already want. Knowing your core offerings alleviates the pressure that most people feel when it comes to sales because you know you're making specific, targeted offers based on someone's needs, goals and interests. Selling becomes fun when you're simply following up with someone to offer them something you know they already want. Actively keep track of your relationships and use your Miracle Hour to move those relationships forward.

This also provides the opportunity to create new products or services based on the market's wants and needs. Are you hearing a lot of questions about a specific topic? Can you put together an offer that current clients can purchase as an add-on to move them forward faster? Take time to assess the gaps in your offer suite and what current customers, past customers or potential customers might need.

Remember, while there may be an endless number of things that you can do during your Miracle Hour, these aren't random acts of sales or marketing. They're highly intentional, relationship-focused activities that lead people to whatever the best next step is for them.

It's time to take action. You don't need a high-quality camera to run a profitable masterclass. You don't have to write a novel to ask for referrals from a customer. You just have to get started. Whether you're sending invitations, preparing for a conversion event or collaborating for visibility, there are limitless auxiliary activities that you can do during your Miracle Hour. Hopefully this gives you some additional perspective on how this can work for you, based on your goals.

Before we dive into Chapter 8, make sure to head to https://www.thekellyroach.com/miracle to grab your complete Miracle Hour toolkit. Not only will you get access to various templates that can support you with conversion event invitations, referral asks and collaborations, but we also break down how to apply the Miracle Hour across roles and departments so that everyone on your team can win together

Chapter 8: Organize to Win

By this point, you're intimately familiar with the Miracle Hour. We have discussed what it is and why it's so powerful. We've examined its core activities, the five different types of sales and how to forge a millionaire's mindset. Now it's time to get your prospect lists organized and make your Miracle Hour happen. To do this, I'd like to introduce the Dream 1000: Your $100 Million Relationship Rolodex.

The Dream 1000

The Dream 1000 is a process for capturing, segmenting and organizing people who you want to become your customers now or in the future. When a business is about to be sold, that business's most valuable assets are its lists of current and past customers and contacts, plus any prospects and the relationships that business has with them. Most small businesses don't have a mechanism for organizing these assets. Depending on the business's history, these lists might exist in multiple places (online or physical), or they might be outdated or half-completed.

The Dream 1000 is a system for managing the relationships in your business. Think of it as a means to organize, segment, qualify and tag leads. This can be as straightforward as a Google spreadsheet or, if you're a tech wizard, a CRM or other database management tool. No matter what tool you use, the most important thing is that you create a process that works for you. This makes executing your daily Miracle Hour much faster and simpler because you're not starting the hour wondering who to reach out to. You simply pull out your Dream 1000 list, identify the segment you're going to focus on and then start right away.

Frequently, entrepreneurs pick systems that are overly complex. They spend countless hours trying to make the system work when it simply doesn't work for them. That's why I recommend starting with a basic spreadsheet.

Order of Action for Daily Sales

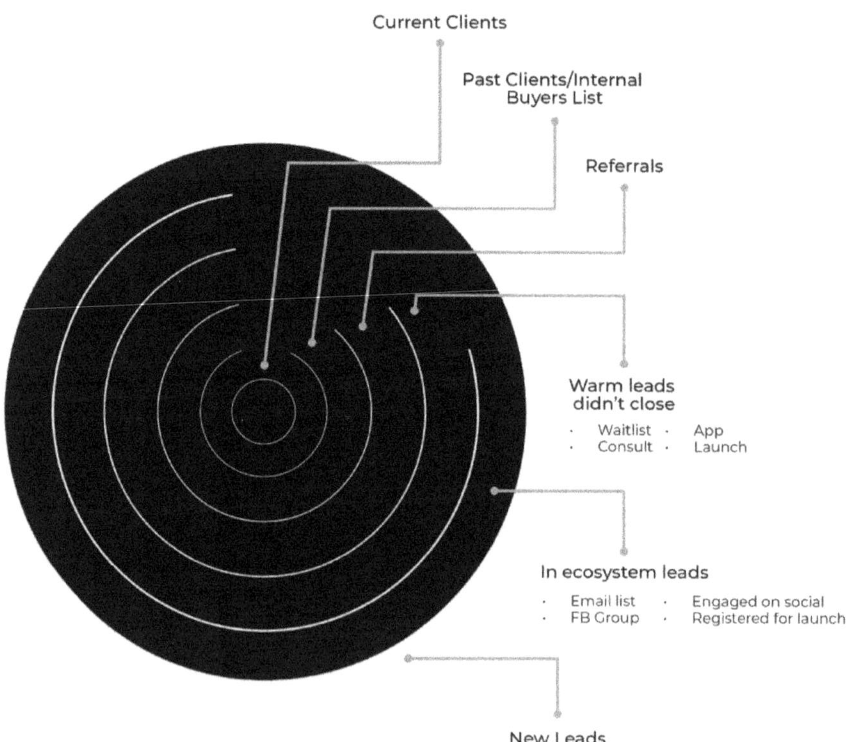

When you put together your Dream 1000, you want to identify and work your warmest leads first and then move out to your coldest. As I've said many times already, your current and past customers are priority #1. From there, we work outward. The illustration on the previous page depicts the order of action for your daily Miracle Hour and the categories you can organize your own Dream 1000 list into.

As you can see, the bullseye is your current customer list. From there, your past customer list. The third ring is for referrals that you've received from clients or peers. Moving outward, you have warm leads, cold leads and finally, the market at large.

Your Dream 1000 should be comprised of a list of people who want, need and can afford your products. Let me emphasize: This is not your whole email list. This is not your whole social media following. This is not every person who's ever opted in for one of your lead magnets. This is not every person who's ever registered for your launch. These are only the people who want, need and can afford your products and services.

The beautiful thing about the Dream 1000 is that it's constantly changing. You may have someone on your "warm list" who has attended multiple conversion events. In the process of executing your Miracle Hour, reaching out, having conversations and qualifying them, you may discover that although they might want or need your offer, they actually can't afford it. Ongoing management of your Dream 1000 means adding and removing people on a day-to-day basis.

In the business world I come from, outside of online marketing, companies would call this a database. Your database is comprised of *targeted, qualified, "best buyers"* that you want to work with. When it comes to online businesses, people tend to treat their *entire* list as their database. On one end of the spectrum, they are trying to interact and manage relationships with everyone, which can quickly become overwhelming and exhausting — especially when those people aren't truly qualified. On the other end, they aren't doing *any* due diligence to identify the most qualified leads on their lists, and never end up pulling those leads through to the sale.

With the Dream 1000, we take the billion-dollar corporate strategy that businesses have used for decades to build wildly successful, publicly traded companies that grow by the millions every year and distill it into a system that small businesses can use to create predictability because it is highly focused and intentional.

Your Dream 1000 will contain segmented lists of qualified leads tagged by specific aspects of your business. There are several ways to do this. First, there are your active and inactive customers (potentially separated by offer, if you have more than one). From there, there are prospects, separated into specific lists based on the product they are deemed a fit for. For example, if you're a media company, maybe you'll have a list of people who have a TV show with the network, a list of people whose podcast you'll produce, a list of people who will publish books with you and so on. These segmented leads live on specific lists based on your team connecting and qualifying.

Let's take a step back before we move forward. Not all leads are created equally. There's a difference between the greater market, which has a general interest in your products, and the *qualified* market, which is in a state of readiness to buy. In the Miracle Hour trainings that my Virtual Business School clients watch, I walk through how to connect and have conversations with leads as they come into their ecosystem so that they can quickly identify whether those leads are *qualified* buyers or not. You'll still engage with your market as a whole, but they might be nothing more than avid fans of the brand, listening to your podcasts, watching your YouTube videos and consuming your content. Or maybe you will take them through the qualifying process, but only your most qualified buyers should have a spot on the Dream 1000.

Are you clear on the top three questions you will use to qualify and segment leads coming into any part of your ecosystem?

Question 1: _______________________________________

Question 2: _______________________________________

Question 3: _______________________________________

If not, I recommend checking out The Virtual Business School. While we focus in-depth on mastering your Miracle Hour and Dream 1000 for consistent, predictable success, you will also get access to qualifying strategies that will help you speed up the process versus wasting time in conversations with those who aren't serious about transformation or are never going to buy. You can visit https://virtualbusinessschool.com to learn more or get started.

> *"The Dream 1000 is blowing my mind. I have so many people I can qualify!"*
>
> *-Anonymous Virtual Business School Member*

The reason we call it the Dream 1000 is because ultimately, you're shooting for 1,000 names on your list per person on your team. If 15 people on your team are running a Miracle Hour, you'd ultimately have 15 lists of 1,000 names. There are roughly 20 business days in a month. If you have 1,000 people on the list, every person on the list should hear from your company at least twice a month. The Dream 1000 is how you take a 10-year goal and achieve it in six months or less with consistency, frequency and quality.

During your Miracle Hour, make it a goal to touch 100 people each day. One hundred people per day becomes 500 a week, which becomes 1,000 over a two-week period. So each qualified lead hears from your company at least twice a month. Why is this crucial? The vast majority of sales happen between the eighth and 12th touch, and most people never get anywhere near that amount of contact. That's why their business doesn't grow. That's why they swim in mediocrity at the top of the funnel. That's why so many entrepreneurs work 80 hours a week while their businesses still aren't making daily sales.

The Miracle Hour and the Dream 1000 work together: The Miracle Hour is for the actions you'll take and the Dream 1000 is for the people on which you'll focus those actions.

Qualifying Your Dream 1000

The quickest way to qualify someone is to ask about their previous investments in the industry or space that you are selling in. Inevitably, the person will share their investment life story and by the end, you can gauge whether they're a qualified buyer or not. The rule in selling is 80% listening, 20% talking. Asking a prospective buyer questions about their behavior will help you understand what they've done in the past, helping you predict what they'll do in the future. Their answers will also allow you to determine what level they are at and which product, program, investment tier or service they might qualify for. Ask open-ended questions and people will tell you everything you need to know.

What open-ended questions can you or your team ask to best qualify leads as they enter your ecosystem?

1: ____

2: ____

3: ____

Contacting People on Your Dream 1000 List

If someone is on your Dream 1000, they should be a recipient of any form of contact or communication you prioritize during your Miracle Hour. For instance, if you're sending out invitations to a workshop or masterclass, include the people on your Dream 1000 who are a fit for that specific offer. If you're working through your inbox or DMs, send them DMs. If they've requested information but haven't taken action, follow up to get a call booked or to reactivate the conversation. Once a person is on the Dream 1000, you should ideally include them in all of your Miracle Hour activities on a two-week rotation like I mentioned before.

The Dream 1000 is set up to touch every single person on your list over a two-week period so that you can be in touch with every targeted prospect twice each month. If there's someone you'd like to work with and no one in your organization is staying top of mind at least twice a month, their buying cycle will open and close. They'll make a buying decision before you've had a chance to reach out or follow up. You'll miss the opportunity without even knowing it.

Disqualifying Your Dream 1000

Most entrepreneurs have a tendency to remove people from their target list far too early and for the wrong reasons. They don't want to be rejected. They might also think no response means "no" when, in actuality, the best buyers typically respond the least. Why? Because they're busy!

Chatty Cathy is the person who has loads of time to chat your ear off but usually cannot afford your services. Though you might believe she's your best lead because she's your most engaged lead, often Chatty Cathy has no money. She has time to talk to you, but she has no money. On the other hand, Busy Bob, who never responds, is actually working on growing his business. Therefore, if you want Busy Bob's business, you have to follow up diligently.

Before removing anyone from your Dream 1000, do a quick refresh of the sales statistics I keep mentioning. It takes 20-40 impressions to get someone's attention. It takes 8 to 12 follow-ups and four no's to get to a yes. Repetition is key, which is why I keep repeating these statistics. If you don't understand sales mechanics and logistics, and you're acting based on emotion, you'll eventually stop following up with the right people and continue following up with the wrong people.

Again, there are occasions when people should be removed from your Dream 1000. In my businesses, there are two reasons this happens. First, if the individual states that they have absolutely no interest in our product, service or program, or they'll never invest, they are removed from our list. Second, if a person directly requests to be removed from the list, we do so. Of course, if they completely disqualify themselves because their situation has changed or they do not meet our ideal client criteria, we remove them.

Building Your Dream 1000 Pipeline

I've worked with thousands of entrepreneurs over the years, and I've seen it time and time again: When people start the process of building out pipelines based on their Dream 1000, they feel completely overwhelmed. Why? Most people start from zero. They don't have updated lists of their current and past customers, let alone any sense of how to go about effectively compiling and maintaining those lists. But I'm here to reassure you that you can tackle this, even if you're beginning at zero. I've seen people succeed when they're starting from square one countless times. Earlier in the book, I shared a saying that applies here as well: Dance where your feet are. Start from where you are, with what you have.

> *"In just under an hour, we not only designed the structure of my personal Dream 1000 database, but also a complete daily workflow for The Miracle Hour, which I can use to start from scratch, take my first steps, add new leads as I gain experience, refine my appraoch, and get better every day.*
>
> *THANK YOU for this great opportunity to integrate these two powerful concepts into my spiritual selling process."*
>
> *-Anonymous Virtual Business School Member*

The first step is listing out your categories: active customers, inactive customers, target lists by product and connections you want to advance (i.e, you don't know enough about them yet to categorize them properly). As you start, it might take a bit to get your footing, but once you find a rhythm, you'll discover that there are leads and opportunities everywhere.

While initially you may find yourself overwhelmed or frustrated by the pace (getting to 1,000 seems impossible at first), within a week or two you will realize how many opportunities you have. In fact, you'll see nearly limitless potential for sales: people in your text message replies; people responding to your emails; people in your DMs; people who booked a call but didn't buy; people who opted in for specific resources, workshops or trainings; and people with whom you need to schedule a follow-up call. You have leads and opportunities everywhere, but since they're not organized right now, you aren't set up to win.

That all changes now. Again, if you'd like more support with getting your Dream 1000 organized to win, we help clients with this daily through The Virtual Business School. You can get started now by visiting https://www.virtualbusinessschool.com.

> *"Celebrating 3 weeks of daily Miracle Hour, leading to 6 sales, 3 in my trust builder, 3 in a mid ticket private, just shy of 14K contracted sales. I've compiled a comprehensive list of all my past clients and have an organized dream 1000 spreadsheet template that is now personalized.*
>
> *It felt gawky at first but now I am in flow and am doing the daily reps with a clear intention of filling it in with 1000 qualified names of people I'm in rapport with, regardless of how long it takes, because I see how this will become the most valuable asset for the stability and sustainability of my business!"*
>
> *-Anonymous Virtual Business School Member*

In getting organized, you bring a sense of purpose to your Miracle Hour. You might decide to focus one day on inactive clients. The next day you'll review inactive customers, and the next you'll reach out to those inactive customers with a welcome-back offer. Another day is for focusing on an upcoming retreat. And then another day is for personally inviting 10 seven-figure business owners to that retreat. See how the momentum builds?

Once you've built your lists, make an inventory of the places you can source leads and past customers from. Tackle this one platform or CRM at a time. Where are the people who booked calls on Calendly but never showed up? That's a list right there. Where do you keep track of people who attended your launches but didn't buy? That's another list. Who commented on your posts for lead magnets in ManyChat? Another list. Who in your Stripe account has purchased an offer from you in the past? Whether it was a $10 subscription, a $17 guide, a one-off intensive, or a 6-

month program. I absolutely recommend that your Dream 1000 also include a list of people who attended a consultation for a high-ticket service and didn't buy. If they were interested enough to give you an hour of their time, follow up.

Organization is everything. Organization drives speed, speed and efficiency allow you to create top-of-mind awareness, and top-of-mind awareness is what drives sales. Just remember, organization is not synonymous with advanced or complicated tech. It can be simple. I've seen some of the most profitable businesses use Google Sheets to keep track of important data. I don't consider myself especially tech savvy. Frankly, I can barely figure out how to operate the remote control at home. And yet, I can build a multimillion-dollar business with my eyes closed.

So open a Google Sheet, start listing out those names by category and organizing your tabs. This will make your Miracle Hour run seamlessly. If you want to get fancy later, you can eventually start tracking everything in a CRM. While today my teams have smart lists and documentation in our own CRM, that's not what makes the strategy successful. Our success is the byproduct of discipline around daily activities.

This brings me to my final point. In coaching clients over the years to build seven- and eight-figure businesses, I've observed that 80% of sales success comes from discipline of execution. It's not about years of experience or talent. It's about discipline and consistency. No wonder so many entrepreneurs grow frustrated and disappointed. No wonder they find themselves asking, "Why is this person more successful than me? They don't have a quality product. They're not doing good work." There is one answer: Execution. It's a level playing field for everyone, but you have to get out of your comfort zone and execute.

List the categories of your Dream 1000 list. For example, active clients by program, inactive clients by program, consult calls, referral partners, potential new clients by offer, etc.

1: ____

2: ____

3: ____

4: ____

5: ____

6: ____

7: ____

8: ____

9: ____

10: ____

Notice how, once again, our lists also mirror the five types of daily sales — upsells, renewals, reactivations, referrals and new customers? Notice how this *also* mirrors the order of activity?

Reactivations
Referrals
New Prospects
Renewals
Upsells
(internal buyers list or
program uplevel)

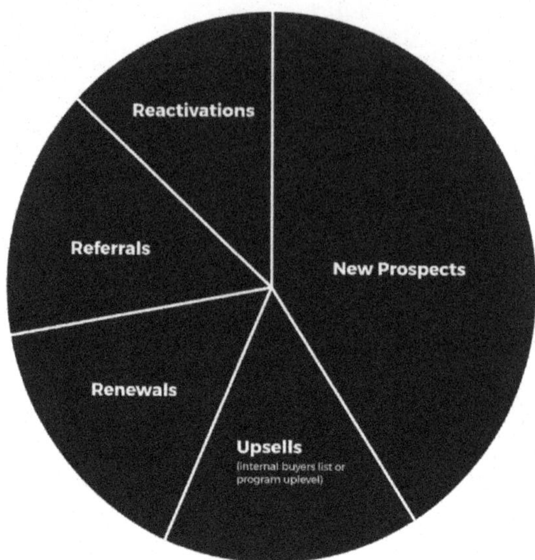

Figure 8.1

Order of Action for Daily Sales

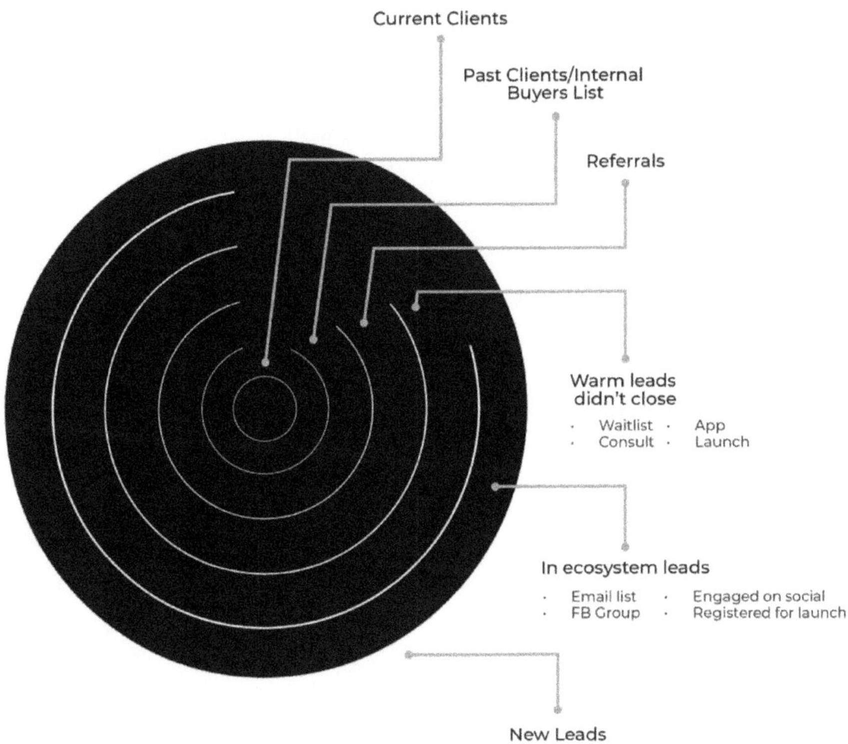

The Power of Predictability

One of the most valuable things you can build into your business is an ecosystem that supports sales to come from multiple directions all the time so you aren't reliant on any one source. I've had my Facebook account hacked and shut down; I've had my LinkedIn account shut down; I've had my Instagram account accidentally suspended and then (thankfully) reinstated. If you've been in business for any number of years, you know nothing is stable. Control is a myth.

That's why having a spreadsheet with names and contact information — phone numbers and email addresses of your prospects — is so critical. You don't own any social media platform. You are on rented land, land that can disappear when you wake up tomorrow. But if you have the contact information for your customers and your leads, it doesn't matter. You harness the power of predictability. And that is the ultimate goal of the Dream 1000: Predictable, perpetual sales, everywhere.

Start where you are with what you have. Go one by one and take inventory of all the places that you may have leads. Think of all the ways that you interface with the market on a daily basis, all the people who have ever expressed interest in your freebies, products, programs and services. Once you start identifying where those leads are, you will see the momentum and velocity build as they become part of your Miracle Hour process.

Use the Dream 1000 Asset Inventory to conduct an asset inventory. List out all the places you can quickly pull from to identify your 1,000 best leads.

Remember to audit:

- All previous calendar bookings to identify past calls that didn't close (Calendly or another booking software you use)
- Manychat for leads who commented or direct messaged you for access to specific freebies and offers
- CRM tools that give insight into the stages of prospects in your pipeline (i.e Grouptrack) – consider tags from past workshop or launch registrations, newsletter signups, or lead magnet opt-ins

- Stripe or payment processor/merchant account for both small and significant payments – from books and bundles, to courses and programs
- The "Contact us" form on your website
- Past referrals from clients that were introduced to you but never connected or closed
- Phone contacts
- Email and text replies
- Direct messages, story mentions, message requests folder, and comments from recent posts – who is reaching out to you on social?
- Facebook group members (from current groups or past popup groups)
- Top engaged subscribers (email, Substack)

Just because leads exist in these places does not automatically qualify them for your Dream 1000. It is up to you to do your due diligence and make sure that they want, need, and can afford your services before adding them to the list. This is simply a recommendation of places to double-check and ensure no leads fall through the cracks.

DREAM 1000 ASSET INVENTORY

Lead source	Notes
Ex: workshop registrations	All leads from past 6 month workshops
Ex: Lead magnet downloads	
Ex: Past clients	

Remember that this strategy is adaptable across departments, and every role might have a slightly different variation of the Dream 1000. For example, marketing may focus on managing leads that are newly following you on social media and requesting resources on specific posts (with a primary goal of managing pull-through from social to email list). Sales, on the other hand, may mainly involve working the new leads that enter your ecosystem. Client services should largely focus on existing clients and referrals.

If you're curious about how your own team can structure their Dream 1000 and Miracle Hour, make sure to grab the Miracle Hour toolkit by visiting https://www.thekellyroach.com/miracle. Inside, we break out activities and focus per role and department so that everyone in your organization can work together to target various areas of the business and win as a team.

Chapter 9: Marketing is Not Sales

Many entrepreneurs are stuck in the trap of constantly marketing their business. I call this the hamster wheel from hell. On the hamster wheel from hell, entrepreneurs spend all their time and money doing *more*: creating more content, posting more on social media, sending more emails. But again, *more* doesn't lead to more activation. One of the main reasons businesses fail is business owners burn out. And one of the main causes for business owner burnout (which leads to cash-flow issues) is obsessively marketing without any strategy for converting that marketing into sales.

I want to help you avoid this trap altogether. But if you find yourself currently stuck in it, consider this chapter a lifeline and an injection of hope. I promise: You can get off the hamster wheel from hell.

Let's go back to basics and define the difference between marketing and sales. When I explained this to my daughter, Madison, I drew a funnel on a sheet of paper. The job of marketing is to get new people into the top of the funnel. The job of sales is to bring people from the top down to the very bottom of the funnel and get them to the close.

This seems straightforward enough, but I'd wager that 99% of businesses focus on getting people to the top of the funnel without having a strategy for moving people down. What do they do instead? They keep bringing more people into the funnel. They grow their email lists, social media followings and brand presence. Then they wonder, "Why am I working harder and longer and making less than I did as an employee?" The answer is clear: They don't understand the difference between sales and marketing.

The job of marketing is to create brand awareness and brand visibility. Marketing's job is to introduce you to the world. Good marketing generates leads and creates demand. If someone who didn't before know your name now knows your name, thank marketing. Of course, marketing goes beyond awareness and exposure. If marketing does a good enough job, it gets people interested and excited enough about you and your work to interact with the brand.

That's the next step in marketing: Leading a prospect to take some small action. That might be joining your email list, following you on social media or opting in for a promotion you're running. Great marketing even drives direct sales conversions of low-ticket products.

Sales, on the other hand, is the relationship-building process that happens after a lead comes into your world, is consuming your content and has taken one or more high-intent action. It occurs after someone knows your name and has expressed initial interest. The vast majority of small businesses have a great strategy for marketing and no plan for sales, so all their hard work is for naught. You might have 100,000 people on your email list, but if there's no activation — no offers being made or consistent follow-up happening — that list is useless. Marketing can support sales, but marketing can't *make* the sales for you (unless you sell exclusively low-ticket at scale). Sales still have to make sales.

Why is there so much confusion about this relationship? Why are so many entrepreneurs baffled by how to get marketing and sales to work together? I trace the confusion to the early days of online marketing. Back when social media was exploding, there was a lot of cash being pumped into the markets, and an abundance of people were investing loosely. Marketing blurred over the line into sales, and a lot of entrepreneurs started relying on their marketing to do the selling for them. Because it was period of rapid growth, many entrepreneurs got away with that for a long time.

That didn't last forever, though. In fact, this is a major reason why my marketing agency changed its business model to become hyper-selective about only working with seven- and eight-figure entrepreneurs. In the past, business owners hired our agency to generate thousands of leads for them. But business owners and their teams weren't following up on those leads to convert them, and then they would get frustrated that sales weren't coming directly from our efforts on social media. Now we're up-front. We tell clients we can't help them if they're not willing to meet the marketing with a conversion strategy that bring their leads full circle. A lot of people maintain a mindset that marketing will do the selling for them, and it doesn't work (unless, again, you exclusively sell low-ticket offers at scale).

In 2024, we saw the highest business closure rate in many years. As the economy has normalized, inflation has gone up, discretionary spending has gone down, incomes have stagnated and people are reverting to a more normalized way of buying.

We are now doing business in an era where the barrier to enter is ZERO. We have been operating over the last few years in a trust recession, however, the onset of the age of AI is now triggering a brand new set of challenges. The AI world has begun ushering in the era of activation, which we'll talk more about as we progress throughout the book. In this era, marketing alone no longer guides purchasing decisions, especially when it comes to premium buyers. Instead, customers want to interface with a brand.

In the activation era, buyers are making high-ticket purchases based on relationships. They want to know and trust the person they're working with. They want to feel the human presence behind the product or service they're investing in. Removing the human element is what has caused many businesses, and small businesses in particular, to struggle.

And, it's only getting worse: According to the 2025 Imperva Bad Bot Report, automated bots now account for more than half of all internet traffic at 51% – the first time bots have outnumbered real humans online in a decade – and that number is only expected to grow.

AI is accelerating at a rapid pace, and most businesses are racing to chase the latest tools and trends. However, the data points toward something different:

Global data and market research company Nielson cites that 92% of consumers trust recommendations from people they know above other forms of influence – and in high ticket sales, that trust is often the deciding factor.

Research from Alden Investment Group shows that 85% of high net worth clients prefer working with advisors and partners who were referred by someone in their inner circle.

Close rates are exponentially higher when they come from referrals or intimate, highly-curated settings.

Businesses are unknowingly charging toward their own extinction by outsourcing and chasing AI, while premium buyers are moving money decisions offline entirely. Smart founders, on the other hand, are quickly realizing that they can set themselves for success by learning how to manage and multiply one of the few things AI cannot replace: relationships.

The Miracle Hour is the Missing Link
In 2025, the Miracle Hour saved countless businesses. That's not because it's an earth-shattering strategy or because I'm the greatest coach in the world. It's simply because the Miracle Hour helps establish the connection between sales and marketing. During the Miracle Hour, you take the hard work your marketing is doing (which is generating leads and providing opportunity) and transform that into income by activating those people through direct interface.

Say social media marketing is consistently driving people to follow your accounts, engage with your content and join your email list. During your Miracle Hour, sales need to close the deal. Remember, in today's world, that doesn't mean scheduling lunches or even cold-calling. It can be a direct message, a text message or a one-minute audio message. It can be inviting people to join you live for a masterclass or a launch. It doesn't need to be an arduous task. That's what's beautiful about the concentrated focus of the Miracle Hour: One dedicated hour prevents you from becoming overwhelmed and succumbing to business owner burnout.

The Miracle Hour is designed to touch the top, middle and bottom of the funnel, killing the feast-or-famine quality of business forever. It is key that you select five to seven activities for your own Miracle Hour that touch all segments of your funnel: top, middle and bottom.

Understand the Difference Between Organizing and Executing
When people exhaust themselves with marketing, they're left without any energy for selling. This is where I observe the distinction between organizing versus *executing*. The majority of people who start the Miracle Hour spend the whole 60 minutes tinkering and trying to decide who to contact. By the end of the hour, they've contacted maybe three people. Remember, organizing is setting yourself up to win; executing is taking action.

I tell my team that before they start a Miracle Hour, they should know who their 100 targets are for the day. The easiest way to do that is to pick specific lists from your Dream 1000 so that your work is streamlined. In other words, go down the same list with the same offer or the same objective.

For example, I might focus today's Miracle Hour on filling events. Tomorrow, I'll focus on consulting offers. The next day, I'll focused on filling our group coaching program and the next day, I'll focus on filling our mastermind. When you make your Dream 1000 and break it down by offer, targeting 100 people a day with similar messaging becomes incredibly repeatable.

Each stage of the Miracle hour can be applied to each list. You connect with potential prospects for that list or offer, post content as it relates to that offer or topic, engage on the content with the top 20 people you want to close for that offer, reply to post threads related to that offer, sweep your inbox and reactivate past conversations about that offer, go live about that offer, and make 20 direct invitations to that offer. Even with a different list to focus on every single day, the activities don't change.

As I shared in the previous chapter, my team keeps a spreadsheet. We use CRMs but bear in mind that all CRMs have their own unique issues, just as all tech platforms have issues. We've had entire lists or tags disappear. The key thing I've learned is that your list is your top asset. Back it up and maintain it in multiple places for insurance and peace of mind.

A common misconception is that an email list is your number one asset. It's not. I could have 100,000 people on my email list, and that list could be making me $0. Your email list is only as effective as you are at stewarding your email list. (And this is coming from someone who makes sales from their email list each day.)

On the other hand, your Dream 1000 is invaluable. It's the future of your business because it's the list that you integrate on a day-to-day basis. It's not just a list of people who you are mass marketing to. Remember, marketing is about simply reaching people in volume. The Miracle Hour is about doing the unscalable in a structured, repeatable way that can be replicated by anyone in your organization.

No matter what type of business you're trying to build, understanding the difference between sales and marketing is crucial for long-term success. Marketing's job is to get people into the top of funnel; sales' job is to move them down the funnel to close. Finally, remember the difference between activity and activation. Be sure that the human side of your business meets and marries the tech and automation side to create truly sustainable outcomes.

Want to make sure your full sales and marketing ecosystem is working? Make sure to review the Miracle Hour steps by role and department with the Miracle Hour toolkit: https://www.thekellyroach.com/miracle.

Chapter 10: The Five Phases of the Miracle Hour

I often find that when business owners begin implementing the Miracle Hour, they get overwhelmed and often give up before sticking with it long enough to see results because it *feels* like a lot. The Miracle Hour requires mastery that takes time. You may find that when you start, it takes longer than an hour a day to fully execute it. That's common, but the more consistently you stick to it, the faster you'll become.

If you (or your team) begin your Miracle Hour from square one, the most effective method is to break it up into phases that build upon one another. Let's break down what those five phases are so you can start building a daily system that feels manageable and prevents you from giving up prematurely.

Phase One: Building Your List
If you've ever wished for a crystal ball that could predict your business's success and ensure you'll make enough sales to sustain your goals, growth and profitability for life, combining your Dream 1000 with the Miracle Hour is it. Building that $100 Million Relationship Rolodex is your superpower.

Keep in mind that everyone starts from zero. Everyone starts by adding one name to the list. That's what I want you to concentrate on in Phase One. Focus on adding one name at a time.

There are many ways to begin. Let your team help. Maybe it starts by logging into Stripe, exporting a list of past customers and adding them to your inactive list. Maybe it's having your client delivery or operations person gather a list of current, active customers. Maybe it's having your sales team identify everyone they've had consultations with over the last 90 days who were qualified but did not convert. Gather names and contact information, platform by platform, asset by asset. No matter what, do not let yourself get overwhelmed and give up. Every single name you add to this list is a huge win — your first 10 names or your first 100 names. Every name advances the future of your business. It protects and serves your family. It creates an insurance policy for your business. It sets you up for future profitability and success.

Build that list and trust the process. Put one foot in front of the other.

I often remind my clients that businesses are built brick by brick. Everyone wants to fast-forward to the final product, but when you add names to your Dream 1000, you are actively constructing a strong and lasting foundation for your business. You're also creating endless opportunity for growth. There's a reason I call this the $100 Million Relationship Rolodex.

The opportunities to grow are endless, but in order to shatter the ceiling that keeps most businesses stuck below six figures and finally reach seven, eight or beyond, you have to better organize and manage relationships. Lay the bricks, steady the foundation and set yourself up for future success.

Phase Two: Engagement

Let me be transparent: Building your Dream 1000 list to 1,000 may take months. But that hardly means you're stalled in Phase One the whole time. You don't have to finish your list to begin Phase Two. In fact, I advise clients to start Phase Two the moment they have a single name on that list. In essence, Phases One and Two operate simultaneously. Whenever someone is added to your list, begin engaging with them.

What does engagement look like? Connection. It might be as simple as a message on Facebook to say, "Hey, I know we've been connected for years, but you and I haven't talked for months.

I'd love to hear what's happening in your business right now. What are you working on? What are your focus areas for the next year?" When I use the word *engage*, I mean reestablish connection.

For some, this might feel a little awkward. If you go to https://www.thekellyroach.com/miracle and download the toolkit, you'll find a bank of templates for engaging different leads in every category — current clients, past clients, someone you had a previous call with, new leads and new followers — in every scenario and situation. These templates have been proven to work, so there's no fumbling or guesswork required. I am serving real-world business success to you on a silver platter. My aim is to help you cut through the excuses so you can get these people in the 10-day rotation and go.

"I have 50 people now in my trust-building offer, which was my year-end goal!"

-Anonymous Virtual Business School Member

Remember, businesses are built brick by brick. It might take you weeks or months to reach your full Dream 1000. That's OK. You can start making sales from day one with a handful of people on the list, especially if you're starting with current or past customers. Today, you can start making upsells and selling add-ons. You can reactivate past customers. You can engage active clients with a thoughtful voice memo like, "Hey, I'm so happy we get to work together in XYZ capacity. One of the areas that we help a lot of people is through ABC service, but I don't think I've talked about that with you. Is this something you would be interested in exploring?"

With this style of casual engagement, there's nothing "salesy" about the ask. You're simply informing current customers of the full scope of your offerings and sharing all the ways you can help them.

Using your Miracle Hour in conjunction with your Dream 1000, set a goal to ensure you hit those five buckets of sales each week (upselling, renewing, referring, reactivating past customers and selling to new customers). Be sure that both your Miracle Hour activities and your Dream 1000 list include each of these categories. This way, every day you'll have clear direction. If yesterday you made an upsell, today you might focus on a reactivation, and tomorrow you might aim to get a new customer in the door. During Phase Two, you're constantly refining the process and refining your list.

Phase Three: Convert Like Crazy
When you start winning every day, the Miracle Hour gets *really* fun. I don't know any business owners who aren't more excited, motivated, fulfilled, passionate and purposeful in their business than when they score wins every day. The goal of the Miracle Hour is to convert people every day. The singular outcome you want to achieve is making sales every day. You'll start with one sale, then duplicate and multiply.

Converting and seeing an outcome from the Miracle Hour goes back to planning and organization. In other words, to make successful conversions, you need to know before starting the Miracle Hour who your top 100 leads will be for the day, what category of your Dream 1000 you're targeting and what activities you're focused on.

As you continue to execute the Miracle Hour each day, your future pipeline will grow and compound. Eventually, you'll come into each month with a list already established of sales that you anticipate will close because they gave you a timeline and you're in active conversation. This means you're maintaining that relationship and top-of-mind awareness.

Those who implement the Miracle Hour consistently are able to eliminate feast-or-famine issues in their business. By the time you jump into Phase Three, which can realistically be in a matter of days of starting the Miracle Hour process, you should be making daily offers. When you make invitations for people to buy from you each day, something incredible happens: sales, sales and more sales.

The reality is that most business owners are one bad month or two away from either having to lay off their staff or give themselves a pay cut. But the Miracle Hour ensures that cash flow valves from multiple directions work simultaneously every single day to create sustainable and predictable growth in the business. Once you get going with your Miracle Hour and your Dream 1000, this becomes an end-to-end relationship and sales management system. You're building actual, meaningful relationships every day because you are actually getting to know the people on the Dream 1000 list.

> *"I am happy to report that I have closed at least one person every single day for the past 12 days into either my primary trust building offer, or offers that I'm testing.*
>
> *This has NEVER happened before!"*
>
> *-Anonymous Virtual Business School Member*

Enter the six-month pipeline. As your relationships develop, people will share with you their timeline to buy. For instance, a client might say, "I'm really interested in hiring your team to help me scale my business. I have a couple projects that I'm finishing in January and February, but I would love to look at a mid-March start date." Between now and then, you'll stay in touch with that client, and, of course, you'll put their name in your pipeline with a target to close in March.

Instead of leaving that conversation for months, that person becomes part of your two-week rotation. You will follow up consistently — not with a direct offer, as you already know their timeline to buy — simply to stay top of mind. Add value for them, support their work, or ask about their personal life (if you have built that rapport) or how things are going with the projects they mentioned.

The goal is to build real, human relationships. If you know the people on your list — their business vision or what they have going on in their lives — you'll be better able to predict and meet their needs. As you review your Dream 1000 and Miracle Hour each week, you're getting direct feedback from people on your list about their goals, their buying criteria and their timeline. This enables you to build a true pipeline where daily conversations lead to slotting in clients for upcoming months. That way, at the start of a new month, you already have a quality list of people you've been building relationships with who've expressed interest and shared real timelines with you. This isn't a Hail Mary. This is how you build a pipeline. When you hit the first of the month, you'll have prospects teed up. You'll simply reconfirm their interest and determine how soon they can invest.

People appreciate when you take an interest in them. That's why I love the Miracle Hour and Dream 1000: They're both about being human. There are two different ways of selling. There's blunt, aggressive, scripted selling, and then there's the *human* version. I aspire to teach you the human version. When you truly take an interest in selling, asking your potential customer meaningful questions and listening to their answers, you build reciprocity before they've even spent a dollar on you. And that reciprocity pays dividends.

Helping entrepreneurs serve their clients and grow their businesses is the joy of my life. Your vibe attracts your tribe. I believe I attract really good humans, and what I give them are systems and frameworks to reach their potential. I get to watch them come in feeling overwhelmed, not having a system for sales or knowing how to create predictability in their businesses, and then see the transformation firsthand.

For instance, one of my clients recently had her first $1.2 million launch. She revealed that just by investing in my Legacy Leaders Mastermind group, she was able to make $250,000 more than her last launch. That's the work that we do. It doesn't require you to step out of your integrity or displace your values. You can be completely and authentically yourself. It requires running your business based on systems, frameworks, processes, discipline and repetition while focusing on the fundamentals.

Phase 4: Scale Your Sales
Many business owners resist learning and mastering sales. They protest, "I'm not a salesperson. I don't want to be the salesperson." But what I always remind my clients is that developing any skill, whether that be sales or utilizing a CRM, is about learning something so you can transfer it.

I love teaching people to scale their sales. My whole business is teaching people how to sell one-to-many, but you have to walk before you can run. That means you have to install a working sales system like the Miracle Hour before you can *scale* a sales system.

The Miracle Hour and Dream 1000 help people get that foundation in place so they can hand it over to someone else. Multiple people on my team have produced millions of dollars in sales for me. Why? I spent time investing in their development, mentoring and coaching them, and shifting their mindsets in order to get them to embrace sales. They could see that it is the transfer of inspiration and the maximization of human potential. Giving people frameworks and structures will make them successful.

Whether you identify as a salesperson or not, if you want to scale your sales, it starts with having a system and designing the system in a way that can be transferred successfully. Then it can be multiplied and duplicated. This will allow many people in your organization to take that one successful framework and replicate the results.

Sometimes clients will share their anxiety about scaling their own sales. They may be confident selling to one person, but the thought of selling one-to-many (for example, in a launch or masterclass) seems daunting. I reassure these clients that selling to many is a trainable skill and yes, that means you can train yourself, too. I built my business by first selling one-to-one by doing singular consultations on the phone, but there came a point when I needed to maximize my time. That's when I mastered launching and then developed the Live Launch method to teach thousands of people to do the same.

For now, know that if you can sell one-to-one, you can sell one-to-many. Like practically everything in life, it's a matter of repetition. It's about getting comfortable on camera, teaching, serving and making an invitation. Anyone who wants to be successful can learn it.

Phase Five: Reinvest for Industry Leadership

Once you're making daily sales in your business and focused on retaining and serving existing customers, and getting new ones, you'll reach a point where every sale becomes profit. Powerfully, this is when you can reinvest to become a category leader.

What do I mean by that? When I was starting my business, I began by spending $1,000 a month on advertising. I bootstrapped my way, brick by brick, dollar by dollar, to get to $100,000 per month on advertising. One day, hopefully, that will become $1 million per month on advertising. I went from being a nobody to a category leader in the coaching space by sheer consistency and repetition. There were no hacks, no shortcuts, no magic. I ran through the reps. Every six to eight weeks I did a live launch. I'd sell and market every day and share value with the market every day. It didn't happen overnight — nothing does.

All good things that are built to last take time, but they also compound with consistency. Most people who don't have the success they want expect things to happen too quickly, and they stop too soon when they don't see the fruits of their labor. In other words, they don't put in enough reps. It's truly repetition over time that creates momentum and velocity. It's like rolling a snowball.

Most people don't realize that if you're simply willing to do things that most people won't do (repeating the fundamentals and having discipline around a daily sales system) you can become part of the 1% in your industry. A lot of people don't believe that this is possible for them. They don't realize that most folks are swimming around in circles at the bottom of every industry and that there are very few players at the top. You *can* be part of the 1% in your industry. You *can* be a one-in-a-million category leader if you're willing to embrace these principles and cultivate the discipline to scale the unscalable.

When people feel your human touch, when you build relationships, and demonstrate your conviction, confidence, passion and energy, it's contagious. That's what will build a brand.

Overnight success is a myth. Every overnight success is at least 15 years in the making. I tell everybody that I'm a 23-year overnight success. I also tell people not to go into something if they don't plan to commit years to it. If you study the story of any person you admire, you'll observe decades of sacrifice and years of investment and laying bricks.

As I type these words, the world is unpredictable, the business climate is wild and things seem to be shifting and changing each day. This is why it's so critical now to have a sales system that can work on any platform, online or offline, in any market or industry. To thrive in the business world of today, you need pliability and potency. You need a system that is both adaptable and reliable regardless of what is happening in the world around. That system is the Miracle Hour.

Review the five phases of implementing the Miracle Hour and see how fast you can move through them in order to see incredible results in your business:

1) Build your list;
2) Engage;
3) Convert like crazy;
4) Scale your sales; and
5) Reinvest toward industry leadership.

Remember, the building process requires patience, repetition and consistency over time.

Imperfect action paves the way to greatness, step by step you will see the massive opportunities ahead.

If any of these five phases feel confusing or uncertain, or you simply want to surround yourself with other entrepreneurs who are leveraging the same strategy to grow, join our Virtual Business School community. You'll get the accountability, training, support, structure and templates you need to win in all five categories. Visit https://www.virtualbusinessschool.com to learn more or enroll today and receive complimentary access for up to three team members when you join.

Chapter 11: Committing to Win: Mastering Daily Habits That Drive Predictable Growth

Winning and losing with the Miracle Hour is like winning and losing in business in general and, for that matter, in life. It's all about mindset.

Winning is the result of deciding that you care more about achieving the outcome you desire than being comfortable in the moment. It's about having patience. So often, people quit because they're not seeing results as fast as they'd like. Why not build something extraordinary? Why not create a business that you love and that performs and is profitable? A business that wins is one you'll never want to escape. It will be something that you enjoy building. It will create generational wealth and impact far beyond your life. That's what I want to stress: Every sale that you make is a life that you can change. It increases your impact and your contribution to the world.

If you're reading this book, you probably started — or are thinking about starting — a business, because you have something you believe in to your core. Something you know you can contribute. Something that will make the world a better place and help people achieve their potential. Sales are at the heart of that.

And yet, I've coached many entrepreneurs who try to skip the mindset step. What happens? They always end up coming back to it. So why avoid mindset work in the first place? As humans, we do a really good job justifying our own behavior. We believe the stories we tell ourselves without realizing those stories may be keeping us stuck. Remember, if you're working really hard and your business isn't growing, you're working really hard on the wrong things. That can be a tough pill to swallow.

If you're reading this book, you want to win. You may be working hard on your business, but are you working on areas that will create congruence between what you *say* you want in your life and how you show up day to day to become the person that your dreams require?

Our brains like justifications. Take my morning workouts as an example. Every day, I wake up and have everything prepped to exercise. If I don't, I'll get in my own head, and I can give you every reason why I *shouldn't* work out. In business and in life, you have to know where you have tendencies to make excuses or tell stories. My tendency is always to work more. So if I don't have an appointment set with my trainer in the morning, I'll wake up and start working. Instead, I pay thousands of dollars to have the accountability to start my day with exercise because I understand that will impact every other area of my success. In my logical brain, I know that exercise is more important for me than working is, but I also know my own tendencies — and excuses.

I share this as a reminder to everyone reading. If you need help or accountability, if you have great intentions reading this book but your likelihood of implementing it is low, get in touch to learn more about how we can help. Book a call with a member of my team, get a coach or find someone to hold you accountable. That pertains not only to business, but to any area of life.

For more than a decade, we have been helping service-based businesses grow and scale online with simple systems for sales, marketing and building winning, profitable teams. We work with businesses from the startup phase (mastering daily sales and online growth) to those making seven or eight figures who want to scale by learning how to get results through others.

If you are curious to learn more about our programs or custom one-on-one consulting packages, follow the QR code to schedule a call with a member of my team.

Schedule a call with our team

People always say, "I'm working so hard," but hard work doesn't guarantee success. If you're working hard on things that don't move the needle or generate profit, no amount of hard work on the wrong things will get you the right result.

Becoming a role model with the right activities is key, especially if you have a desire to one day monetize and elevate a winning team. Ideally, when you hire someone for a sales role, or any role you would like to monetize for that matter, you have a qualified list and training plan ready to go before they even start. It's not talent, it's intent around time management.

In the 2023 Trends in International Mathematics and Science Study (TIMSS), Japanese students in fourth through eight grade ranked among the top worldwide for math. Some assumed this was because they simply had a stronger propensity for math in that in part of the world. Maybe they were more intelligent. Maybe something about their upbringing or culture was the reason why they were outperforming most of the world in this area. However, after studying the difference between students scoring highly in math versus those who weren't, researchers discovered that the amount of time students spent studying math accounted for the difference in scores. They found that those who spent more time on a task with deeper engagement and focused on solutions, thinking and structured problem solving got better results.

This principle is widely applicable. In business, the chief stressors in any company are growth and customer acquisition. Yet, the time spent constructively solving these problems in a meaningful way is insignificant. Small businesses in particular struggle with founder dependency rather than installing sales systems to break that cycle.

It doesn't matter whether we're talking about athletics, business, music, art or another skill that you're developing. It is said that it takes about 10,000 hours to master a skill. There's a direct correlation between how much time you spend on something (with intention) and your ability to master it. It's not about propensity. It's not about talent. It's not about advantage. We all know people in our lives who have been given every advantage under the sun, and they've done nothing with it.

If you want to utilize your gifts to your highest capability, that also means recognizing when something is within your zone of excellence versus your zone of genius. Many business owners are constantly stuck working in their zone of excellence because it's comfortable. The zone of excellence is where we play to our natural strengths whereas our zone of genius requires us to refine our gifts, work hard and challenge ourselves to step outside of our comfort zone to become everything we're capable of being.

Building winning teams typically requires you to step out of your zone of excellence, whether that be you doing it yourself or falling back on old strategies that have always worked. Stepping into that zone of genius means declaring, "I have a bigger vision for my life. I have a bigger vision for my business. I'm willing to run the reps, stretch myself and get uncomfortable as I become the person that my dreams require."

The truth is, anyone can achieve a 10-year goal in six months or less with the right systems in place.

One of the most important lessons of my entire working career came from my very first entry-level position in the Fortune 500 world. I worked for a company that stipulated we could only sell within our designated zip codes.

Now, being confined to a designated zip code meant that there was an extremely limited number of companies for me to sell to in order to achieve the level of growth that would yield me the promotion I was seeking. I was given the territory of West Chester, Pennsylvania, which also happens to be the home of the shopping channel QVC. Right away, the team sat me down and told me not to bother selling to them. "Don't even put QVC on your list," they said. "You'll never get in — we've been trying for 10 years."

Well, you better believe that meant I was committed to finding a way to work with QVC. I made the decision that I would be the one to change that story. How? It started with identifying the activities I knew would increase the likelihood of taking that 10-year failure and turning it into a success:

1) Consistency. Was I committed to calling, emailing and delivering marketing materials to the QVC team consistently?

2) Frequency. How often was I willing to do this? In the past, it was done on and off for a decade. I decided I would get in front of them every single week.

3) Quality. How was I going to improve the effectiveness of the contact that I had with them to make a greater, and faster, impression?

You can take any 10-year goal and achieve it in six months or less if you look at these three criteria: consistency, frequency and quality. Lo and behold, within about six months, we partnered with the one and only QVC. Never let someone else's lack of ambition cause you to lower yours.

What is a 10-year goal that you need to start taking seriously? If you were to look at consistency, frequency and quality as the three power levers that you can adjust starting now to achieve that 10-year goal in six months or less, what actions do you need to take today?

____

____

____

____

____

____

Start with one building block at a time. For instance, with fitness, I started with 30-minute sessions three times a week, and that proved life-changing. For anyone reading this book, just start. Or as I always say, just pick up the dumbbell.

Maybe you start by devoting 30 minutes a day to a few texts or DMs or a phone call here and there. Suddenly, you'll realize that what you viewed as Mount Everest standing between you and your dreams was nothing but a molehill you could conquer with one hour a day.

The Miracle Hour Toolkit
People generally have good intentions when it comes to making progress. They start listening to trainings. They decide to do the thing and then gear up. But when they go to send the DM, they feel overwhelmed. They think, "I don't know what to say," or "I don't know how to connect."

As I discussed earlier, organization and planning are not synonymous with execution. I don't want you to devote your time and energy to figuring out what to say instead of directing that energy toward connecting with people. That is how the Miracle Hour can change your life, and it's why I built the complete toolkit for you. You can access it for free at https://www.thekellyroach.com/miracle.

The Miracle Hour toolkit is a treasure trove of resources created and maintained by my team. I have a team that executes the Miracle Hour every single day, and by this point, it should be abundantly clear that we live, breathe, eat and sleep these principles. No matter what your specific situation or scenario is, chances are we've dealt with it and overcame it. The toolkit exists so that rather than spending your time on organization or trying to figure out what to say, you can go out and meaningfully connect using the resources we've provided. You've got every tool necessary to take action, so no excuses.

You'll get access to our complete Miracle Hour guide, which outlines the seven core activities and what it takes to be successful, scripts, templates and word tracks for each stage of activity, and how to structure a Miracle Hour by team role or department. Scan the QR code to get access for free.

Grab The Miracle Hour Toolkit

The Importance of Follow-Up

By now, you know that follow-up is where the majority of sales happen. However, most people never follow up more than once. This takes them out of the game completely, and it's why so many business owners burn out before they ever scale up.

This is a tragedy to me, especially with burnout among entrepreneurs being a crisis of epic proportions. One of my biggest motivations for writing this book was to combat some of that burnout. I know why entrepreneurs are suffering. I have spent over a decade working intimately with entrepreneurs across industries and in over 30 countries. I'm here to tell you that most entrepreneurs spend more than half of their work week "working hard" on things that are meant to sidestep or facilitate the sales process indirectly when that could be consolidated into just a handful of hours per week of direct profit-producing activities. Imagine how life-changing it would be to free up 25 hours each week for your family, faith, fitness, hobbies, fulfilling projects and friends.

Fortune is in the follow-up. All the money is in the follow-up. Let's be honest: How seriously do you take someone who gets in touch with you once and never contacts you again? I'm certainly not doing business with that person. If someone doesn't have the level and caliber of professionalism in conducting business when you haven't paid them yet, I'd be terrified to see what their follow-up is like once you *do* pay them. (Spoiler alert: It doesn't get better. It gets worse.) Think about the impression you're setting in terms of the kind of professional you are and the way you interact with people. The tone you set before you do business is what people will expect after you do business. If you're chaotic, inconsistent, infrequent or random in how you connect with them, there's a very low likelihood that the best buyers will want to work with you.

As I mentioned before, the best potential clients are usually the busiest ones. If you assume that prospects will sell themselves into your offers, that is not a great business strategy. I personally do not believe that we are entitled to anything. We are not entitled to someone doing business with us just because we had a single interaction with them.

> *"Since jumping in a month ago, I've brought in 15 new clients into my Trust Building Offer and one into my signature program...this is the standard I want to have moving forward to keep building on.*
>
> *Finally feel like I'm breaking my 4-minute mile."*
>
> *-Anonymous Virtual Business School Member*

Another piece of the follow-up process is giving people the chance to experience multiple interactions with you and ultimately decide whether or not they want to do business with you. People underestimate this. They believe that just because a person follows them on social media and engages with their content, or signs up for their launch, that all of a sudden that person should give them their money. Trust is built over time and through repeated interactions. The faster you demonstrate consistency and frequency in adding value for the people that you'd like to do business with, the easier it will be for your sales and success to compound.

Commit to win. That's neither a talent nor skill; it's a decision. If you're reading this and ready to commit to a simple but intentional strategy, I invite you to join the Virtual Business School. While this book is a great starting point for taking action with a daily Miracle Hour, the Virtual Business School provides the accountability, space and support to execute consistently over

time so that those results can compound. Visit
https://www.virtualbusinessschool.com.

Chapter 12: Multiply and Scale

As you build your Dream 1000, you'll deepen and strengthen relationships. After all, that's the whole point of the Dream 1000. Relationships fuel the Miracle Hour, which means that you'll be able to take your ever-growing list and divide and conquer.

As your business grows and you generate sales, you can take what you've designed with the Miracle Hour and begin teaching it to more people in your organization. The fastest, easiest way to grow and scale your company profitably is to hand someone a list of warm leads from day one and tee them up to win right away.

In teaching, coaching, and consulting on sales, I recognize that often what happens is businesses hire salespeople and those salespeople come in completely cold. They have no database. There's no organized plan. They spend months on end just creating their own list. This is one of the reasons why small businesses especially have such high turnover rates with salespeople. Around months three or four, the business owner gets frustrated that the salesperson isn't closing or making any money and they decide to let them go.

What a mistake. It typically takes three to four months to get a pipeline tight, clean and working with enough repetition to where it's driving consistent sales. Many small business owners don't understand that building these out is the hardest and most time-consuming part of setting up a salesperson for success in the form of daily sales. Here they are firing the salesperson, when actually they should be firing themselves. After hiring hundreds of salespeople in my own corporate career, helping larger companies install sales systems and now teaching small business owners, I've seen the same trend spread from Fortune 500 companies to midsize and small businesses. It plays out the same way every time, every place.

So how do you set up your company to duplicate and multiply without it being reliant on you? You do that by creating systems and processes then building talent and tenure with the right people. The Miracle Hour and Dream 1000 can be a huge piece of this. If you can set a salesperson up for success by handing them a warm, qualified list from day one, that salesperson goes from being an expense to being an income generator from the get-go. Anyone who has hired people understands what I'm talking about. People are your biggest expense. The more you take your payroll from an expense to an investment by helping your people become profitable, the faster and easier it will be to scale because now you have more manpower. This time, though, it's not costing you money, it's making you money.

If you continue to build the Dream 1000 list, you'll reach a point where inevitably you'll have overflow. That's a good thing. Start to separate out that overflow. Build and keep those leads warm so that they are ready for the next person to come in and completely transform your business and your life forever because now you have the ability to multiply and scale while retaining profit margins.

Businesses fall into a "valley of death" because, often, they can't afford to float the expenses during the time between starting a new strategy and profiting off that strategy. People are your biggest strategy, and they're also your biggest expense. By learning to use the Miracle Hour system to shorten the time around making people profitable in your business, you'll win immediately.

Look at this through the lens of client services, customer support, sales and marketing — frankly, every role in your company. Since four of the five types of sales that you want to make every week are contingent on your current customers, the Miracle Hour and Dream 1000 is not something that is specific to your sales team. This is for everyone and anyone who is marketing and growing your brand, especially the people who handle client services or interface with current and past customers.

> *"I and my team finally implemented The Miracle Hour a few weeks ago after learning and hearing about it for months! We're seeing the results coming in and this is going to create a snowball effect. We used to depend on paid ads and live launches, but we decided to stop it for one month and go all in to The Miracle Hour. Not only we saved thousands of dollars on ads, the quality of leads and conversation is so much better. We have more than $100K in the pipeline and it's a matter of time when this is going to explode!"*
>
> *-Mamiko Ito, Business Mentor, Founder & CEO of Mamiko Ito Consulting,*

Setting your people up for success from day one should be non-negotiable. Whether or not you do this will make or break your company. You won't be able to scale a company if you cannot monetize your people. If you're leaving it up to your people to figure this out for themselves without preparing them for that challenge — right as they're also learning a new company, culture and role — you've failed. It's too tall an order for someone who just joined your team. The fastest, easiest way to give yourself that insurance policy for profitability is to set up new hires for success and build their confidence from day one.

Employees are like athletes. When an athlete builds their confidence, they play harder, run faster, get better results and win more often. Employees are exactly the same. When you tee them up for success, help them achieve a quick win or build their confidence, they'll perform at a higher level, producing bigger and better results for you.

This, in part, is why I run the Miracle Hour with my own team. To be clear, there's absolutely no need for me to be on a Zoom call with them each day as they're doing the Miracle Hour. They already know how to do it. I don't manage my own Dream 1000 list, and I am no longer the primary sales engine for the company. I was when I developed the Miracle Hour and back when I was following the activities on my Magic Index Card. Now, I've duplicated and multiplied so that I have a team of people doing this across multiple companies of mine.

Today, as CEO, my most important job is casting vision, instilling confidence and leading the team to success. What does attending their Miracle Hour every day signal to the team? It tells them that it's important, and that it's a priority. My attendance keeps the trains on the tracks.

So many CEOs and small business owners see a little bit of success and quickly drift too far from what's happening with the business. When suddenly that progress and those margins disappear, it can take weeks or years to get a business back on track. As a CEO, staying connected to your people, to the market and to your clients is essential for long-term success.

When you run a Miracle Hour for a team, ask yourself what you can do to make it faster and easier for them to win? When I run a Miracle Hour with my team, I often come with templates, maybe some hooks and angles for them to use, focus suggestions and opportunities for quick wins. When I attend, I try to give my team those advantages — whether that be a tool or a resource — that will speed up their progress or results.

Frankly, if you're running a Miracle Hour for yourself, it shouldn't be much different. You prepare for that time by having your templates ready, knowing who you'll target, deciding what conversation you'll have and maintaining focus. Growth is driven by intent, not just activity. Too often, people miss the *intent* part.

***

You can make your dreams come true. Nothing is out of reach for you and nothing is impossible with God. However, as Saint Augustine said, "God provides the wind, but man must raise the sails."

Whatever goal, vision or dream you have, you can make it happen. Looking back on my life, from the free lunch line to becoming a God-made multimillionaire, I can honestly say that the Miracle Hour was a huge piece of making that happen. This extraordinarily and undeniably simple system can be your bridge to freedom. My wish, my hope and my goal for you reading this book is that you realize that if you take back your time, if you claim ownership of your future, if you allow your focus to remain fixed on the things that matter, you can make your dreams come true.

> *"Miracle Hour wins for February:*
> *3 VIP days booked, $300K closed*
> *in sales, [and] 2 live, paid speaking*
> *events booked in Italy for 2026!"*
>
> *-Maria Fontana, Founder at*
> *Maria Fontana Consulting*

For the better part of a decade, I provided only high-ticket coaching and consulting for tens of thousands of dollars to elite entrepreneurs. In doing so, I was able to have a front-row seat to leaders making six-, seven- and even eight-figure leaps in their businesses. But a few years ago, God called me to provide accessible, real-world business education that absolutely anyone around the world could afford if they were serious about their dream.

Enter the Virtual Business School. The Virtual Business School is a real-world accountability, education and implementation community that is focused on helping leaders and their teams install a predictable daily sales system in their businesses. We teach real-world, cutting-edge sales and marketing strategy that works, plain and simple.

This incredible program includes:
1) Live masterclasses

2) Ongoing real-world business and sales trainings
3) Accountability structure
4) Live Q&A and hot-seat coaching
5) Community

Throughout the program, you are reminded over and over again to take back your power, retain a simple focus and put the Dream 1000 and Miracle Hour to work in your business. Inside the Virtual Business School, we have six- to nine-figure business leaders and their teams participating in the Miracle Hour and actively building their Dream 1000 lists. One of my main missions in life is to help more leaders build seven- and eight-figure businesses that allow them to put their faith and their families first. This also requires a system for breaking founder dependency, which is why we so strongly encourage you to enroll your sales and marketing team in the Virtual Business School. We can remove that weight from you and directly empower them to support you in building the dream, and when you enroll, you get complimentary access for up to three team members to help make that happen.

> *"Virtual Business School nails the framework for entrepreneurs to set up shop and immediately start serving their markets.*
>
> *Having spent most of my career in the large global sales/marketing space and then made the pivot to be in business for myself, I found that I had a lot to re-learn. Virtual Business School made it easy and fun."*
>
> *-Anonymous Virtual Business School Member*

I can't wait to help you fulfill your highest potential and make your dreams come true with Virtual Business School. Visit https://www.virtualbusinessschool.com to learn more and join us now.

As author Cal Newport revealed in his book *Deep Work: Rules for Focused Success in a Distracted World*, one focused hour of deep work is roughly equivalent to a full eight-hour distracted workday. Some say even that is an understatement. The Miracle Hour can and will change your life if you allow it to.

So the only question is: How badly do you want it?

END

Are you ready to join the Virtual Business School and unlock your next million-dollar breakthrough? Scan the QR code and join hundreds of entrepreneurs who are building wildly simple, profitable businesses by harnessing the power of our three-part sales system: Miracle Hour, Dream 1000, and "easy yes" Trust Building Offers.

Join The Virtual Business School

These wildly simple strategies are available to you (and your team) to get started right away. When you join the Virtual Business School, you will start by completing a short onboarding form that gives us a glimpse at where you are in your business currently and of your goals. From there, we will schedule a short onboarding call to get acquainted and point you toward the resources that will make the most meaningful difference for you right way based on your current stage of business and goals.

We recommend all business owners and teams start by reviewing our three-part system and clearing their calendars to attend our monthly live calls. We meet virtually each week for implementation sessions to hold you accountable to executing your Miracle Hour, with new templates, hands-on support and guidance, and live accountability. Again, visit https://www.virtualbusinessschool.com to get started.

About Kelly Roach

Kelly Roach is a Former NFL Cheerleader and Fortune 500 executive turned entrepreneur who has taught over 100,000 entrepreneurs how to build wildly successful and profitable businesses online.

As the founder and CEO of Kelly Roach International, Kelly helps entrepreneurs around the globe master sales predictably, profitably and integrity online. Her first company reached over eight-figures in the online space, and she now runs a portfolio of companies focused on helping entrepreneurs scale their sales and grow their empires, all while putting their faith and families *first*.

Her podcast, The Kelly Roach Show, has reached the top 1% in marketing shows globally with over 1,100 episodes and nearly 1,000 reviews. Her companies have been featured on the Inc. 5000 List of Fastest Growing Private Companies in the United States multiple years in a row and have been featured by major publications and television networks, including Forbes, INC., ABC, NBC, Fox and more. Kelly has been Titan's Coaching CEO of the Year, received a Women in Business Stevie Award and was named to Inc.'s Best in Business.

Her mission is simple: To help you achieve your dreams without sacrificing the most sacred parts of life — faith, family, fitness, freedom and fulfillment.

Connect with Kelly on Socials:

Substack:

https://kellyroachofficial.substack.com/

Instagram:

https://www.instagram.com/kellyroachofficial/

Facebook:

https://www.facebook.com/kelly.roach.520/

LinkedIn:

https://www.linkedin.com/in/kellyroachint/

Sign up for The Sacred Art of Selling book waitlist:

https://thekellyroach.com/bts